GRAMMAR 101

FROM **SPLIT INFINITIVES** TO **DANGLING PARTICIPLES,**
AN ESSENTIAL GUIDE TO **UNDERSTANDING GRAMMAR**

KATHLEEN SEARS

ADAMS MEDIA
NEW YORK   LONDON   TORONTO   SYDNEY   NEW DELHI

Adams Media
An Imprint of Simon & Schuster, Inc.
100 Technology Center Drive
Stoughton, MA 02072

First Adams Media hardcover edition MAY 2017

ADAMS MEDIA and colophon are trademarks of Simon and Schuster.

For information about special discounts for bulk purchases, please contact Simon &
Schuster Special Sales at 1-866-506-1949 or business@simonandschuster.com.

The Simon & Schuster Speakers Bureau can bring authors to your live event. For more
information or to book an event contact the Simon & Schuster Speakers Bureau at
1-866-248-3049 or visit our website at www.simonspeakers.com.

Interior design by Colleen Cunningham

Manufactured in the United States of America

9 2023

Library of Congress Cataloging-in-Publication Data has been applied for.

ISBN 978-1-5072-0359-0
ISBN 978-1-5072-0360-6 (ebook)

Contains material adapted from the following title published by Adams Media, an
Imprint of Simon & Schuster, Inc.: *The Everything® Grammar and Style Book, 2nd
Edition* by Susan Thurman, copyright © 2008, ISBN: 978-1-59869-452-9.

CONTENTS

CHAPTER 4: MAIN PARTS OF SPEECH 99

CHAPTER 5: PRONOUNS 127

CHAPTER 6: ADDITIONAL PARTS OF SPEECH 151

CHAPTER 7: TENSES AND FORMS 169

CHAPTER 8: PHRASES, CLAUSES, AND SENTENCE STRUCTURE   191

CHAPTER 9: CONSTRUCTING COHERENT SENTENCES   215

CHAPTER 10: MISTAKES AND MISUSED PHRASES   255

APPENDIX: ROOT WORDS, PREFIXES, AND SUFFIXES   272

INDEX   282

INTRODUCTION

Think grammar and spelling aren't important? Then you should consider this:

- A misplaced comma on the Tariff Act of June 6, 1872, cost the United States government an estimated $2 million in revenue
- A missing hyphen in a NASA document forced the destruction of a billon-dollar satellite that was meant to collect data on Venus
- A missing word in a 1631 printing of the Bible promoted rampant promiscuity

As these examples show, correct grammar is essential for proper communication and understanding. If you use grammar incorrectly, it reflects badly on your speaking and writing skills—and it may cause others to doubt your reliability. Proper English grammar, correct English grammar, is a vital matter. But what exactly is grammar?

The study of language began around the sixth century B.C. in both Greece and India. Indian scholars concentrated on transmission of Sanskrit while the Greeks focused on the study of written language. Both Plato and Aristotle took an interest in this study of language and provided the discussion for the concept of parts of speech. The Greek scholar Dionysius Thrax even wrote a grammar text of sorts entitled *The Art of Letters* that discussed the nature of letters, syllables, and word forms. Thrax's work laid the basis for many of the grammar concepts we still hold to today.

English grammar, our standard set of rules for spelling, punctuation, and sentence structure, had its beginnings in the Middle Ages. At this time, the English language had no standard or regulation and had become the third language in its own country—it was essentially a language of the lower classes. In fact, there were so many regional dialects of English at this time that people in one part of England could not understand people from neighboring regions—even one as close as 50 miles away. By the 1600s, this lack of consistency made people believe that the English language was not as "good" as French and Latin and that it needed to be improved. As a result, the first English grammars were created.

The first attempts at codifying an English grammar were based on Latin grammar, but these versions often fell short because many of the nuances of English could not be made to follow Latin's grammatical rules. However, in 1775, when Samuel Johnson published his *Dictionary of the English Language*, the rules for standard English grammar were finally established, leading to effective communication across all the people of England.

By the end of that century an American named Lindley Murray published the most prominent and influential work on English grammar. Murray's book—*English Grammar Adapted to the Different Classes of Learners*—was not just a description of grammar but rather a kind of handbook for how to write proper English. Following Murray's lead, many other volumes on grammar followed—including Noah Webster's *A Grammatical Institute of the English Language*, which became the backbone of American education and taught more than five generations of children the rules of spelling and grammar. By the nineteenth century the rules of English grammar were widespread—from schools, houses, and universities to newspapers and books—and proper grammar had finally taken hold.

Yet despite its pivotal importance, many people still see grammar as a difficult and taxing subject to learn. While it is true that grammar is a large topic with many rules and even some exceptions, *Grammar 101* simplifies the topic for you and gives you an easy-to-understand survey of English grammar rules. Whether you have struggled to master grammar in the past or are just interested in learning all you can about this nuanced and fascinating discipline, this straightforward guide will take you step by step through all the skills you need to learn, including:

- Understanding the individual parts of speech and elements of a sentence
- Using the correct punctuation in your sentences
- Avoiding the most common grammatical, spelling, and writing mistakes

With hundreds of concrete examples that show you the correct and incorrect ways to construct clear and eloquent sentences, you'll learn how to write and speak with confidence. This book has all the ingredients you need to master grammar and become a great communicator.

So whether you're looking to fill in some holes in your knowledge, get a refresher on what you learned in high school or college, or are merely supplementing an English course you're taking, *Grammar 101* has got you covered. From misplaced commas, problems with agreement, and trying to figure out things like whether you should use *effect* or *affect*, this guide will walk you through each problem situation and show you the correct path to choose.

Chapter 1

Spelling

Today, with the proliferation of computers and technology in our world, people have come to rely on their devices to tell them if a word is spelled correctly. As long as they run a spell check and no words come up, most people assume everything is accurate and spelled correctly. But computer-based spell checkers are not always accurate—after all, a computer spell checker is essentially a lexicon (a list of words). The computer compares your word against its list of properly spelled words, and if it doesn't match it simply gives you an error message. Sometimes your computer will offer suggestions on how to spell a word, but these are simply based on similarities between your word and the computer's list of words. The meaning may be completely different. Computer spell checkers give a false sense of security. Nothing can match the ability of knowing some basic spelling rules, such as using root words and mnemonics, and of course reaching for a good dictionary. Let's begin our explorations into the wonderful world of grammar and style with the most elemental unit through which you communicate meaning: the word. A single word includes a world of significance—so make sure you spell it correctly!

SPELLING BASICS

Every Rule Has an Exception

Nearly 90 percent of English words can be spelled correctly if you know the basic spelling patterns and rules. You probably remember a few rules about spelling from your elementary-school days. The poem that most students deem unforgettable is this one:

> *I before e,*
> *Except after c,*
> *Or when sounded as <u>a</u>,*
> *As in <u>neighbor</u> or <u>weigh</u>.*

That's certainly a helpful mnemonic—most of the time. It works for words such as *beige, ceiling, conceive, feign, field, inveigh, obeisance, priest, receive, shield, sleigh,* and *weight.*

But take a look at these words that don't follow the rule from the poem: ancient, caffeine, codeine, conscience, deify, deity, efficient, either, feisty, foreign, forfeit, height, heist, kaleidoscope, leisure, nucleic, protein, reimburse, reincarnation, science, seize, sleight, society, sovereign, species, sufficient, surfeit, and weird.

You see enough exceptions to wonder about the rule, don't you?

There are also other common spelling rules including:

- Silent e helps a vowel say its name: This means when a word ends with a vowel followed by a consonant and then silent e, the vowel has a long sound (this is the reason for the differences in rate and rat, fine and fin, cube and cub).
- When two vowels are together, the first one does the talking: Meaning the first vowel in a vowel pair will be long (the sound is the same as the sound of the letter) and the second vowel will be silent (for example, meat, seat, rain, goat).

- Most nouns become plural by adding –s, except for those that end in ch, sh, s, x, or z—those become plural by adding –es.

However, memorizing rules is not the most effective way to learn spelling as most rules have exceptions.

Grammar Facts

You do know, of course, not to rely on the spell-check feature of your word processor to catch all your spelling mistakes. Off coarse ewe due. Ewe no the programme that ewe ewes two cheque mite look threw and thru an knot find awl your miss takes. An it wont tell ewe what ewe kneed too change the word two.

Here are some rules that generally apply to English nouns. (Note the word *generally*.) English has adopted words from many languages, and those languages have differing ways of changing word forms. That means, unfortunately, that every rule will have an exception (and probably more than one, as you've seen). Although the whole enchilada can be pretty confusing, the information you'll learn in this chapter will provide you with some useful guidelines for making your spelling decisions.

AMERICAN VERSUS BRITISH SPELLINGS

You probably know the meanings of some words are different in Britain than in the United States, such as the British usage of *chips* for what Americans call *French fries* and *lorry* for what Americans call a *truck*. But are you aware that the two languages have many variations in spelling as well? Here are a few of the spelling differences between American English and British English words:

AMERICAN ENGLISH	BRITISH ENGLISH
airplane	aeroplane
annex	annexe
center	centre
check	cheque
color	colour
cozy	cosy
curb	kerb
draft	draught
gray	grey
jail	gaol
licorice	liquorice
maneuver	manoeuvre
mold	mould
plow	plough
spelled	spelt
smolder	smoulder
theater	theatre
tire	tyre

Grammar Facts

Our present-day study of grammar and spelling descends from the Greeks. While many philosophers such as Plato and Aristotle studied grammar and language as it related to logic, our grammar system was first founded by Dionysius Thrax, who wrote about letters, syllables, complex word forms, and more in his work *The Art of Letters*.

FORMING PLURALS

Is It Potatos or Potatoes?

Let's say you're making a list of items from your home to take to a local charity. Are you donating two chairs or two chaires? three clocks or three clockes? five knives or five knifes? a picture of six deers or a picture of six deer? You get the picture; plurals in English are formed in any number of ways.

1. To form the plural of most English words that don't end in -s, -z, -x, -sh, -ch, or -ss, add -s at the end:

    desk = desks, book = books, cup = cups

2. To form the plural of most English words that end in -s, -z, -x, -sh, -ch, and -ss, add -es at the end:

    bus = buses, buzz = buzzes, box = boxes, dish = dishes, church = churches, kiss = kisses

    Exceptions to this rule include *quizzes, frizzes,* and *whizzes.* (Note the doubled -z.)

3. To form the plural of some English words that end in -o, add -es at the end:

    potato = potatoes, echo = echoes, hero = heroes

    To make things interesting, other words that end in -o add only -s at the end:

    auto = autos, alto = altos, two = twos, zoo = zoos

And—just to keep you on your toes—some words ending in -o can form the plural in multiple ways:

buffalo = buffalo/buffaloes/buffalos, cargo = cargoes/cargos, ghetto = ghettos/ghettoes

When in doubt about which form to use, consult your dictionary (check to see if your instructor or company prefers a particular dictionary) and use the plural form listed first.

4. To form the plural of most English words that end in a consonant plus -*y*, change the *y* to *i* and add -*es*:

lady = ladies, candy = candies, penny = pennies

5. To form the plural of most English words that end in a vowel plus -*y*, add -*s*:

joy = joys, day = days, key = keys

6. To form the plural of most English words that end in -*f* or -*fe*, change the *f* to *v* and add -*es*:

knife = knives, leaf = leaves, wife = wives

Some exceptions to this rule (didn't you know there would be exceptions?) include *chef, cliff, belief, tariff, bailiff, roof,* and *chief.* All simply add -*s* to form their plural.

7. Some words form their plurals in ways that defy categories:

child = children, mouse = mice, foot = feet, person = people, tooth = teeth, ox = oxen

And—to confuse matters further—some words are the same in both singular and plural:

deer, offspring, crossroads

Grammar Facts

What's odd about these nouns: ides, means, mathematics, outskirts, goods, economics, cattle, clothes, alms? They're among the nouns that don't have a singular form.

Many words that have come into English from other languages retain their original method of constructing plurals:

Latin
- one alumnus = two alumni
- one radius = two radii

Greek
- one analysis = two analyses
- one diagnosis = two diagnoses

These are just some of the rules of spelling, but you'll find lots of others. Many Internet sites are devoted to spelling rules. Just type in "English spelling rules" on a major search engine, and you'll get scores of hits.

CREATING SPELLING MNEMONICS

Give Your Memory a Jump-Start

Let's face it—sometimes spelling rules just don't sink in. The English language has too many rules, and almost all of them have so many exceptions that learning them may not seem worth your time or trouble. So how can you learn to spell properly? Many people create mnemonics (memory aids) to help them spell correctly. Listed here are some commonly misspelled words and suggested mnemonic forms to help you remember the right spelling.

Grammar Facts

A mnemonic is a specific restructuring of content to tie new information more closely to your existing knowledge and therefore aid in your retrieval of that new knowledge. In essence if you can tie the correct spelling of a difficult word to something you already know you will be more likely to remember how to spell the word. For example, an *island* "is land" surrounded by water.

After looking at these mnemonics, try developing some of your own for words that you often misspell (of course, look up the words in the dictionary first to get the right spelling). For mnemonics for some commonly confused words, see the last section in this chapter.

- **abundance:** Is it *-ance* or *-ence*? Remember: "An abun<u>dance</u> of people can <u>dance</u>."
- **ache:** Remember the first letter of each word of this sentence: "<u>A</u>ches <u>C</u>an <u>H</u>urt <u>E</u>verywhere."
- **acquire:** Most misspellings omit the *c*. Remember: "I want to <u>AC</u>quire <u>A</u>ir <u>C</u>onditioning."
- **across:** One *c* or two? Remember: "Walk <u>across a cross</u> walk."

- **address:** One *d* or two? Remember: "I'll <u>add</u> you to my <u>add</u>ress book."
- **aisle:** Remember the first letter of each word of this sentence: "<u>A</u>thletics <u>I</u>n <u>S</u>tadiums <u>L</u>ooks <u>E</u>asy."
- **Arctic:** Remember the first letter of each word of this sentence: "<u>A</u> <u>R</u>eally <u>C</u>old <u>T</u>ime <u>I</u>s <u>C</u>oming."
- **believe:** Remember: "Don't be<u>lie</u>ve a <u>lie</u>."
- **business:** Remember: "I often take the <u>bus in</u> my <u>busin</u>ess."
- **calendar:** Remember: "J<u>A</u>nu<u>A</u>ry is the first month of the c<u>A</u>lend<u>A</u>r."
- **cemetery:** Remember: "<u>E</u>pitaphs are in a c<u>E</u>m<u>E</u>t<u>E</u>ry."
- **defendant:** Remember: "At a picnic, it's hard to <u>defend</u> an <u>ant</u>."
- **dilemma:** Remember: "<u>Emma</u> faced a dil<u>emma</u>."
- **doctor:** Remember: "Get me to the doct<u>OR</u> <u>OR</u> else!"
- **environment:** Remember: "Lots of <u>IRON</u> is in the env<u>IRON</u>ment."
- **equivalent:** Remember: "Is <u>ALE</u> the equiv<u>ALE</u>nt of beer?"
- **escape:** Remember: "It's <u>es</u>sential to <u>es</u>cape."
- **especially:** Remember: "I <u>ESP</u>ecially enjoy <u>ESP</u>."
- **exceed:** Remember: "Don't exc<u>EED</u> the sp<u>EED</u> limit."
- **expensive:** Remember: "Those <u>pens</u> were ex<u>pens</u>ive."
- **familiar:** Remember: "That <u>liar</u> looks fami<u>liar</u>."
- **February:** Remember: "<u>BR</u>r, it's cold in Fe<u>br</u>uary."
- **generally:** Remember: "The gener<u>al</u> is your <u>ally</u>."
- **grammar:** Remember: "Bad gram<u>MAR</u> will <u>MAR</u> your chances for a good job."
- **handkerchief:** Remember: "<u>Hand</u> the <u>chief</u> a <u>hand</u>ker<u>chief</u>."
- **hindrance:** Remember the first letter of each word of this sentence: "<u>H</u>al <u>I</u>s <u>N</u>ot <u>D</u>riving <u>R</u>ight <u>A</u>nd <u>N</u>obody <u>C</u>an <u>E</u>xplain."
- **hoarse:** Remember: "When you're h<u>oarse</u>, you feel as if you have <u>oars</u> in your throat."
- **indispensable:** Remember: "That <u>sable</u> coat is indispen<u>sable</u>."
- **knowledge:** Remember: "I <u>know</u> that <u>ledge</u> is dangerous."

- **loneliness:** Remember: "ELI is known for his lonELIness."
- **maintenance:** Remember: "The main ten student workers got an A in maintenance."
- **maneuver:** Remember the word is spelled with the first letter of each word of this sentence: "Mary And Nancy Eat Ugly Vegetables—Even Radishes."
- **marriage:** Remember: "You have to be a certain age for marriage."
- **mortgage:** Remember: "Mort thought his mortgage rate was a gag."
- **niece:** Remember the first letter in each word of this sentence: "Niece Irma Expects Cute Earrings."
- **parallel:** Remember: "Two parallel lines are in the middle of parallel."
- **peculiar:** Remember: "That peculiar fellow is a liar."
- **rhythm:** Remember: "Two syllables, two hs."
- **roommate:** Remember: "Two roommates, two ms."
- **separate:** Remember: "There's A RAT in separate."
- **sincerely:** Remember: "Can I sincerely RELY on you?"
- **skiing:** "SkIIng has two ski poles in the middle."
- **subtle:** Remember the first letter of each word of this sentence: "Some Ugly Boys Threw Logs Everywhere."
- **surprise:** Remember: "U R surprised when you receive a sURprise." (Sound it out!)
- **villain:** Remember: "A VILLAin is in this VILLA."
- **Wednesday:** Remember: "Try to wed on Wednesday."
- **weird:** Remember the first letter in each word of this sentence: "Weird Eddie Is Really Daring."
- **wholly:** Remember: "HOLLY is in wHOLLY."

PREFIXES, SUFFIXES, AND ROOT WORDS

Get to the Root of the Problem

A number of the words you use today are shaped from prefixes, root words, and suffixes that originally came from many other languages, especially Latin, Greek, Old English, and French. By learning some of these, you can analyze unfamiliar words, break them down into their component parts, and then apply their meanings to help unlock their definitions.

Root words (base words) can add either prefixes or suffixes to create other words. Take, for instance, the root word *bene*, meaning *good*. If you add various prefixes (letters that come at the beginning of a word) and suffixes (letters that come at the end of a word) to *bene*, you can create other words such as *benefit*, *benevolent*, *benediction*, and *unbeneficial*. Each prefix and suffix has a meaning of its own, so by adding one or the other—or both—to root words, you form new words. You can see the root word *bene* in each of the new words, and each of the new words still retains a meaning having to do with *good*, but the prefix or suffix changes or expands on the meaning. (The prefix *un-*, for instance, means "not." That gives a whole new meaning—an opposite meaning—to the word *unbeneficial*.)

Grammar Facts

Interesting, too, is the way ancient word forms have been used to create words in modern times. Two thousand years ago, for instance, no one knew there would be a need for a word that meant *sending your voice far away*—but that's what the modern word *telephone* means. It's a combination of *tele*, meaning *distant or far away*, and *phon*, meaning *voice or sound*.

In another example, look at the root word *chron*, which comes from Greek and means *time*. Adding the prefix *syn-* (meaning *together with*) and the suffix *-ize* (meaning *to cause to be*) creates the modern word *synchronize*, which means *to set various timepieces at the same time*. Use a different suffix, *-ology*, meaning *the study of*, and you have *chronology*, which means *the study that deals with time divisions and assigns events to their proper dates*.

PREFIX AND SUFFIX TIPS

Here are some rules for spelling words to which prefixes or suffixes have been added.

1. Words that end in *-x* don't change when a suffix is added to them:

fax = faxing, hoax = hoaxed, mix = mixer

2. Words that end in *-c* don't change when a suffix is added to them if the letter before the *c* is *a, o, u,* or a consonant:

talc = talcum, maniac = maniacal

3. Words that end in *-c* usually add *k* when a suffix is added to them if the letter before the *c* is *e* or *i* and the pronunciation of the *c* is hard:

picnic = picnickers, colic = colicky, frolic = frolicking

4. Words that end in *-c* usually don't change when a suffix is added to them if the letter before the *c* is *e* or *i* and the pronunciation of the *c* is soft:

critic = criticism, clinic = clinician, lyric = lyricist

5. Words that end in a single consonant immediately preceded by one or more unstressed vowels usually remain unchanged before any suffix:

debit = debited, credit = creditor, felon = felony

Of course, you'll find exceptions, such as:

program = programmed, format = formatting, crystal = crystallize

6. When a prefix is added to form a new word, the root word usually remains unchanged:

spell = misspell, cast = recast, approve = disapprove

In some cases, however, the new word is hyphenated. These exceptions include instances when the last letter of the prefix and the first letter of the word it's joining are the same vowel, when the prefix is being added to a proper noun, and when the new word formed by the prefix and the root must be distinguished from another word spelled in the same way but with a different meaning: anti-institutional, mid-March, re-creation (versus recreation).

7. When adding a suffix to a word ending in *-y*, change the *y* to *i* when the *y* is preceded by a consonant:

carry = carrier, irony = ironic, empty = emptied

This rule doesn't apply to words with an *-ing* ending:

carry = carrying, empty = emptying

This rule also doesn't apply to words in which the *-y* is preceded by a vowel:

delay = delayed, enjoy = enjoyable

8. Two or more words that join to form a compound word usually keep the original spelling of each word:

    cufflink, billfold, bookcase, football

9. If a word ends in *-ie*, change the *-ie* to *-y* before adding *-ing*:

    die = dying, lie = lying, tie = tying

10. When adding *-full* to the end of a word, change the ending to *-ful*:

    armful, grateful, careful

COMMON SPELLING MISTAKES

Choose the Right Word

Need a little advice (or should that be *advise*?) about when to use certain words? Are you feeling alright (or *all right*?) about your ability to distinguish between (or is that *among*?) *alumni, alumnae, alumnus*, and *alumna?* Could you use an angel (or an *angle*?) on your shoulder to give you some guidance? Are you anxious—or are you *eager*?—to overcome your brain freeze about when to use particular words?

Not to worry! This section contains an extensive list of words that are commonly misused or confused. Also included are a number of mnemonics to help you remember the differences when this book isn't handy (although you *should* carry it with you at all times!).

Here are the words that cause some of the greatest amounts of perplexity and befuddlement:

- **a, an:** Use *a* before words that begin with a consonant sound (*a* pig, *a* computer); use *an* before words that begin with a vowel sound (*an* earring, *an* integer). The sound is what makes the difference. Write *a habit* because *habit* starts with the *h* sound after the article, but write *an honor* because the *h* in *honor* isn't pronounced (the first sound of *honor* is the vowel *o*).

  What an honor and a privilege it is to meet a history expert like Prof. Maltby.

- **a lot, alot, allot:** Okay, let's begin with the fact that there is no such word as *alot.* If you mean a great number of people or things, use *a lot.* Here's a mnemonic for this: "a whole lot" is two whole words. If you mean *that allocate*, use *allot.* A mnemonic for *allot* is *allo*cate = *allo*t.

Tomorrow night, the mayor will allot a lot of money for various municipal projects.

- **accept, except:** *Accept* has several meanings, including *believe, take on, endure,* and *consent; except* means *excluding.* If your sentence can keep its meaning if you substitute *excluding,* use *except.*

  Except for food for the volunteers, Doris wouldn't accept any donations.

- **adapt, adopt:** To adapt is to change; to adopt is to take and make your own.

  After Mary Elizabeth and Ron adopted the baby, they learned to adapt to having little sleep.

- **advice, advise:** *Advise* is what you do when you give *advice.* Here's a mnemonic to help you remember: To adv*i*se you must be w*i*se. Good adv*i*ce is to drive slowly on *ice.*

  Grandpa tried to advise me when I was a youngster, but I wouldn't listen to his advice.

- **affect, effect:** *Affect* is usually a verb (something that shows action), usually means *change* or *shape,* and—as a verb—has its accent on the second syllable. (There is a meaning of *affect* as a noun, but unless you're a psychologist you needn't worry about it.) *Effect* is almost always a noun meaning *result* or *outcome, appearance* or *impression* (*effect* has a rare use as a verb, when it means *to achieve* or *cause*). One mnemonic to help you remember is this: Cause and *e*ffect (that is, if you want the word that is to be used in this phrase, you want *effect*—the word that begins with the last letter of *cause*).

The effect of the announcement of impending war won't affect Adam's decision to join the military.

- **aggravate, annoy:** If you mean *pester* or *irritate*, you want *annoy*. Aggravate means *exaggerate* or *make worse*.

  Steven was annoyed when his boss aggravated the situation by talking to the press.

- **aid, aide:** If you help, you *aid*; if you have a helper or supporter, you have an aide.

  The aid from my aide is invaluable.

- **aisle, isle, I'll:** An *aisle* is in a theater; an *isle* is an island (a shortened form of the word); *I'll* is short for *I will*.

  I'll walk down the aisle to meet my groom; then we'll honeymoon on a desert isle.

- **all ready, already:** If you mean all is ready, use *all ready*; if you mean in the past, use *already*.

  I already told you we're all ready to go out to dinner!

- **all right, alright:** *All right* is always two words, although you often see the incorrect spelling *alright*. You wouldn't say something is *aleft* or *alwrong*, would you? (Please say you wouldn't!)

  Is it all right if we eat in tonight?

- **all together, altogether:** *All together* means *simultaneously* or *all at once*; altogether means *entirely* or *wholly*. If you can substitute *entirely* or *wholly* in the sentence and the meaning doesn't change, you need the form of the word that is entirely, wholly one word.

You're altogether wrong about the six friends going all together to the dance; each is going separately.

- **alumni, alumnae, alumnus, alumna:** You can thank the Romans for this confusion; Latin has separate words for masculine, feminine, singular, and plural forms. Here's the rundown: One male graduate is an *alumnus*; one female graduate is an *alumna*; several female graduates are *alumnae*; and several male graduates or several male and female graduates are *alumni*. You can see why the short form *alum* is often used informally; when you use it, you don't have to look up the right form of the word.

Although Mary Jo and her sisters are alumnae from Wellesley, Mary Jo is the alumna who receives the most attention; her brothers Martin and Xavier are alumni of Harvard, but Martin is a more famous alumnus than Xavier.

- **allusion, illusion:** An *allusion* is a reference; an *illusion* is a false impression. If you want a word that means mistaken idea, you want *illusion*.

Kay told Jerry that she was under the illusion he'd be her Prince Charming; Jerry didn't understand the allusion.

- **altar, alter:** If you change something, you alter it; you worship before an *altar*.

We'll alter the position of the altar so the congregation can see the new carvings.

- **among, between:** Think division. If only two people are dividing something, use *between*; if more than two people are involved, use *among*. Here's a mnemonic: be*tw*een for *two* and amon*g* for a *g*roup.

  The money was divided between Sarah and Bob; the land was divided among Billy, Henry, and Lillian.

- **angel, angle:** An *angel* has wings; the degree of an *angle* is often studied.

  The angel's wings are set at ninety-degree angles from its body.

- **anxious, eager:** These two words are often confused. If you're *anxious*, you're nervous or concerned; if you're *eager*, you're enthusiastic.

  I had been anxious about my medical test results, but when they proved negative I was eager to kick up my heels.

- **anybody, any body:** *Anybody* means *any one person* (and is usually interchangeable with *anyone*). *Any body* refers (pardon the graphic reference) to one dead person.

  Anybody can help to search for any body that might not have been found in the wreckage.

- **appraise, apprise:** To ap*praise* is to give value to something (to see how much *praise* it needs); to appr*i*se is to *i*nform.

  The auctioneer called to apprise our family about how he would appraise various items for us.

- **bad, badly:** When you're writing about how you feel, use *bad*. However, if you're writing about how you did something or performed or reacted to something, use *badly* (twisted your ankle *badly*; played *badly* in the game).

  Gregg felt bad he had scored so badly on the test.

- **bazaar, bizarre:** The first is a marketplace; the second means *strange, weird,* or *peculiar*.

  The most bizarre purchase that came from the bazaar was a pair of sandals without any soles.

- **bear, bare:** A b*ear* can t*ear* off your *ear*; if you're bare, you're nude.

  The bare bathers were disturbed when the grizzly bear arrived.

- **besides, beside:** If you want the one that means *in addition to*, you want the one that has an additional *s* (*besides*); *beside* means *by the side of*.

  Besides her groom, the bride wanted her dad beside her in the photo.

- **breath, breathe:** You take a *breath*; you inhale and exhale when you breathe.

  In the cold of the winter, it was hard for me to breathe when taking a breath outside.

- **cavalry, Calvary:** The *cavalry* are soldiers on horseback (the word isn't capitalized unless it begins a sentence); Ca*l*vary is the hi*l*l where Christ was crucified (and is always capitalized).

The cavalry wasn't in attendance for the march up Calvary.

- **can, may:** If you *can* do something, you're physically able to do it. If you *may* do it, you have permission to do it.

You can use "ain't" in a sentence, but you may not.

- **cannot, am not, is not, are not, and all other "nots":** For some strange reason, *cannot* is written as one word. All other words that have *not* with them are written as two words. Go figure.
- **capital, capitol:** The *capitol* is the building in which the legislative body meets. If you mean the one in Washington, D.C., use a capital *C*; if you mean the one in your state, use a lowercase *c*. Remember that the building (the one spelled with an *o*) usually has a dome. Use *capital* with all other meanings.

The capital spent by the legislators at the capitol is appalling.

- **carat, caret, carrot, karat:** A *carat* is a weight for a stone (a diamond, for instance); *carat* is also an alternate spelling of *karat*, which is a measurement of how much gold is in an alloy (as in the abbreviation 18k; the *k* is for *karat*). A *caret* is this proofreading mark: ^ (meaning that you should insert something at that point). Finally, a *carrot* is the orange vegetable your mother told you to eat.

Set in an eighteen-karat gold band, the five-carat diamond was shaped like a carrot.

- **censor, censure:** To censor is to take out the bad material; to *censure* is to place blame (don't cen*sure* someone unless you're *sure*).

The full Senate voted not to censure the senator for trying to censor the email that came to other congressional employees.

- **cite, sight, site:** Your *sight* is your vision or a view (you use your *sight* to look at a beautiful *sight*); to cite is to make reference to a specific source; a *site* is a location, such as on the Internet.

  The colors on the website you cited in your paper were a sight to behold.

- **climactic, climatic:** *Climactic* refers to a climax, a pinnacle; *climatic* is related to the weather (the climate).

  Last year's weather featured many climatic oddities, but the climactic point came when snow arrived in June.

- **coarse, course:** If something is *coarse*, it's rough; *oars* are *coarse*. A *course* is a *route*, a class, or part of the idiomatic phrase "of course."

  The racecourse led the runners over coarse terrain.

- **complement, compliment:** If something completes another thing, it *complements* it (*complete* = *complement*). If you receive praise, you've gotten a *compliment* (*I* like to receive a compliment).

  The jewelry will complement the outfit the star will wear, and she will surely receive many compliments on her attire.

- **conscience, conscious:** Your *conscience* tells you whether something is right or wrong; if you're *conscious*, you're awake and aware.

  On the witness stand, Marie said she wasn't conscious of the fact that her conscience told her not to steal the ashtray from the hotel room.

- **continual, continuous:** *Continuous* actions go on uninterrupted; *continual* actions are intermittent.

  The continual rains lasted for ten days; because of that, the Blacksons had a continuous problem with water in their basement.

- **core, corps, corpse:** A *core* is a center or main section; a *corps* is a group or organization; a *corpse* is a dead body.

  At the core of the Marine Corps corporal's sleeplessness was his discovery of a corpse while on a training mission.

- **council, counsel:** A *council* is an official group, a committee; to *counsel* is to give advice (the stockbroker counseled me to sell).

  The town council decided to counsel the youth group on the proper way to ask for funds.

- **desert, dessert:** A *desert* is a dry, arid place or (usually used in the plural form) a deserved reward or punishment (*just deserts*). The verb that means *to leave* is also *desert*. The food that is so sweet is a dessert.

  While lost in the desert, Rex craved a dessert of apple pie à la mode.

- **device, devise:** A *device* is a machine or tool; to *devise* means *to invent* or *concoct something.*

  To devise, you must be wise. Will this device work on ice?

- **discreet, discrete:** *Discreet* means *cautious, careful,* or *guarded in conduct* (be discreet about whom you meet). *Discrete* means *separate* or *disconnected.*

The dancer's discreet movements were discrete from those performed by the rest of the chorus.

- **dual, duel:** The first means *two* (*dual* purposes); the second is a fight or contest (the lover's jealousy was fuel for the duel).

  The dual reasons for the duel were revenge and money.

- **elicit, illicit:** To elicit something is to extract it, to bring it out; something *illicit* is *illegal*.

  The telephone scam artist engaged in the illicit practice of trying to elicit credit card information.

- **emigrate, immigrate:** To emigrate is to exit a country; to immigrate is to come into a country.

  Ten people were trying to emigrate from the tyranny of their country and immigrate to the United States.

- **eminent, imminent:** Someone well known is eminent; something that might take place immediately is imminent.

  Our meeting with the eminent scientist is imminent.

- **ensure, insure:** To ensure is to make certain of something; insure is only for business purposes (to insure a car).

  To ensure that we continue to insure your house, send payment immediately.

- **everyday, every day:** *Everyday* means *routine* or *daily* (*everyday* low cost); *every day* means *every single day* (low prices *every day*). Use *single* words if you mean every *single* day.

  The everyday inexpensive prices of the store meant that more shoppers came every day.

- **faze, phase:** To *faze* is to *intimidate* or *disturb*. As a noun, a *phase* is *a period of time*; as a verb, it means *to establish gradually*.

  I wasn't fazed by his wish to phase out our relationship.

- **fewer, less:** Use *fewer* to describe plural words; use less to describe singular words.

  The new product has fewer calories and less fat.

- **figuratively, literally:** Literally means precisely as described; figuratively means in a symbolic or metaphoric way.

  When Pauline called, she asked if I was off my rocker; I thought she meant figuratively and wondered why she thought I had gone crazy. However, she intended to be taken literally, as she wondered if I was still sitting outside in my rocker.

- **flaunt, flout:** If you *flaunt* something, you show it off (*flaunt* your new jewelry); to *flout* is to jeer at someone or something in a contemptible way, or to intentionally disobey (*flout* the laws).

  In an attempt to flaunt his new car to the girls on the other side of the road, James decided to flout the law and not stop at the red light.

- **forego, forgo:** If you mean something that has gone be*fore*, use *fore*go (a *foregone* conclusion); if you want the word that means *to do without something*, use *forgo* (the one that is without the *e*).

  It's a foregone conclusion that Meg and Marion will forgo sweets when they're dieting.

- **foreword, forward:** The word that means *the opening information in a book* is *foreword* (it comes be*fore* the first important *word* of the book); for any other meaning, use *forward*.

  To gain insight into the author's intent, you should read the foreword before you proceed forward in the book.

- **foul, fowl:** The animal is a *fowl*; the action on the basketball court is a *foul*; a bad odor smells *foul*.

  The foul smell came from the fowl that had been slaughtered.

- **good, well:** *Good* is an adjective; it doesn't mean in *a high-quality manner*, or *correctly*. If you want either of those meanings you need an adverb, so you want *well*.

  You did well on the test; your grade should be good.

- **graduated, graduated from:** A school *graduates* you; you *graduate from* a school.

  The year Tiya Hudson graduated from college, the school graduated 5,000 students.

- **grisly, grizzly:** A horrible or gruesome sight is *grisly*; the North American bear is a *grizzly*.

A grisly scene was left after the attack by the grizzly bear.

- **heal, heel:** To heal means to cure or patch up (to heal a wound); among other verb definitions, to heel is to tilt to one side, to give money to, or to urge along; a well-heeled person has a considerable amount of money.

  You might need ointment to heal the blisters you get from trying to right the sails when the ship heels in the wind.

- **hear, here:** You h*ear* with your *ear. Here* is the opposite of t*here.*

  Did you hear that Aunt Helen is here?

- **hopefully:** If you mean *I hope,* or *it's hoped,* then that's what you should write. *Hopefully* means *confidently* or *with anticipation.*

  The director waited hopefully for the Oscar nominations to be announced.

- **imply, infer:** Both of these have to do with words not said aloud. A speaker implies something; a listener infers something.

  Rufus thought the boss had implied that she would be back for an inspection next week, but Ruth didn't infer that.

- **in, into:** *In* means with*in; into* means from the outside *to* the *in*side.

  Go into the house, look in my purse, and bring me money.

- **its, it's:** *It's* means only *it is* (before *it's* too late); *its* means *belonging to it* (I gave the dog *its* food and water).

It's a shame the dog lost its bone.

- **lead, led:** If you want the word that means *was in charge of* or *guided*, use *led*; otherwise, use *lead*.

  The company, led by one of the richest people in the world, announced that its CEO was retiring; today a newcomer will lead it.

- **loose, lose:** *Loose* (which rhymes with *noose*) means *not tight*. *Lose* is the opposite of *find* or *win*.

  Will I lose my belt if it's too loose?

- **may of, might of, must of, should of, would of, could of:** In speech, we slur these phrases so that they all sound as if they end in *of*, but in fact all of them end in *have*. Their correct forms are *may have*, *might have*, *must have*, *should have*, *would have*, and *could have*.

  I must have thought you would have been able to find the room without any directions.

- **moral, morale:** If something is *moral*, it's *right* or *ethical* (that's the adjective form); if something has a *moral*, it has a *message* or a *meaning* (that's the noun form). Your morale is your esteem.

  The moral high road that the politician took boosted the morale of the entire staff.

- **myself, itself, yourself, himself, herself, themselves, ourselves, yourselves:** None of these pronouns should ever be used without the antecedent that corresponds to it. You might write:

  I myself would like to go for a drive.

But you shouldn't write, "Mike took Pat and myself for a drive."

- **pacific, specific:** *P*acific means *p*eaceful; *specific* means *precise* or *individualized.*

  To be specific, the pacific view from Hickory Mountain is what calms me the most.

- **passed, past:** *Passed* is a verb; *past* is an adjective (*past* often means *last*) or noun meaning *the preceding time.*

  In the past, twenty parades have passed down this street.

- **peace, piece:** Pe*ace* is the opposite of w*ar*; a *piece* is a part or portion (a *piece* of *pie*).

  The father bargained with his small children, "Give me an hour's peace, and I'll get you a piece of cake."

- **persecute, prosecute:** To persecute is to oppress or bully; to prosecute is to bring legal action.

  We warned our neighbors that we would prosecute if they continued to persecute their dog.

- **pore, pour:** If you *read something carefully*, you *p*ore over it. If you make a liquid go *out* of a container, you p*our* it.

  After Harry accidentally poured ink on the new floor, he pored over several books to find out how to clean the stain.

- **prophecy, prophesy:** You have a forecast or a prediction if you have a prophecy. *Prophesy* is pronounced with the last syllable sounding like *sigh*, and you might sigh when you *prophesy* something dismal.

Last week the audience heard the medium prophesy about forthcoming bad weather; the prophecy has yet to come true.

- **principle, principal:** *Principle* means *law* or *belief*. *Principal* means *major* or *head*; it also means *money that earns interest in a bank*. The princi**pal** is the head person in a school; he or she is your **pal** and makes princi**pal** decisions.

That is the most important principle our principal believes.

- **quiet, quite:** *Quiet* is *calm* or *silence*; *quite* means *to a certain extent*. Be sure to check the ending of the word you use; that's where mistakes are made. Think: I hope my p**et** is qui**et**.

Are you quite sure that you were quiet in the library?

- **real, really:** *Real* means *actual* or *true*; *really* means *in truth* or *in reality*. Except in the most casual tone in writing, neither *real* nor *really* should be used in the sense of *very* (that's a *real* good song on the radio; I'm *really* glad you listened to that station).

When Debbie and Phillip realized they were lost, the real importance of carrying a compass hit them.

- **respectfully, respectively:** If you're *full* of respect for someone and want to show it, you do it respect**fully**. *Respectively* means *in the order stated*.

Upon hearing the news, I respectfully called Bob and Janie, respectively.

- **role, roll:** A *role* is a *position* or *part* (in a production); a *roll* is a *piece of bread* on the dinner table; to *roll* is to *rotate*.

  The role of the acrobat will be played by someone who can perform a backward roll.

- **set, sit:** If you place something, you set it. If you're in an upright position (like in a chair), you sit. In addition, *set* is transitive (it must have an object); *sit* is intransitive (it doesn't have an object).

  Please set the table before you sit down.

- **stationery, stationary:** If you mean something that lacks any motion, use *stationary*; if you mean something you write a letter on, use stationery.

  The stationery had a picture of people riding stationary bicycles.

- **supposed (to):** Often the *-d* is incorrectly omitted from *supposed to* (meaning *expected to* or *designed to*).

  In this job, you're supposed to be able to write short, clear, and effective memos.

- **than, then:** If you mean *next* or *therefore* or *at that time*, you want *then*. If you want the word that shows a comparison, use than.

  For a while, Mary ran more quickly than I; then she dropped her pace.

- **that, which:** For clauses that don't need commas (restrictive clauses), use *that*. For nonrestrictive clauses, which need commas, use *which*.

The local dog kennels, which are nearby, are the ones that have been featured in the news lately.

- **there, their, they're:** If you want the opposite of *here*, use t*here*; if you mean they a*re*, you want they*'re*; if you mean belonging to *th*em, use *th*eir.

  There are employees who think they're going to get their 10 percent raises tomorrow.

- **to, too, two:** If you mean something *additional*, it's the one with the *additional o (too)*; *two* is the *number after one*; *to* means *in the direction of something*.

  Did our supervisor ask the two new employees to go to Detroit and Chicago, too?

- **troop, troupe:** Both are groups of people, but *troupe* refers to actors only.

  The troupe of actors performed for the troop of Brownies.

- **try and, try to:** Almost always the mistake comes in writing *try and* when you need to use *try to*.

  The lady said she would try to get the dress in my size; I hoped she would try and keep looking.

- **weather, whether:** If you mean conditions of the climate, use *weather*. (Can you stand to *eat* in the h*eat* of this bad w*eat*her?) If you mean *which, whichever,* or *if it's true that*, use *whether*.

It's now mid-April, and the weather can't decide whether it's spring or winter.

- **when, where:** If you're writing a definition, don't use either of these words. For instance, don't write "A charley horse is when you get a cramp in your leg"; instead, write something like: "A charley horse is the result of a cramp in your leg."

  A bank is a place in which you can make a deposit or withdrawal.

Grammar Facts

These are considered nonstandard words and phrases (in other words, ones you shouldn't use): *anyways, can't hardly, can't help but, can't scarcely, everywheres, hisself, irregardless, nowheres, off of, theirselves, theirself*—and the number one nonstandard word: *ain't.*

- **who, which, that:** Don't use *which* when you're writing about people. Some style guides have the same restriction for *that* and some don't, so be sure to check.

  The inspector, who gives the orders that we must obey, said that the law, which had never been enforced, would result in higher costs.

- **whose, who's:** *Whose* means *belonging to whom; who's* is short for *who is* (the apostrophe means the *i* has been omitted).

  After the sock hop, who's going to determine whose shoes these are?

- **woman, women:** One *man*, two *men*. One wo*man*, two wo*men*. It's that simple.

  The local woman asked the two visiting women if they'd like a tour of the town.

- **your, you're:** If you mean *belonging to you*, use *your* (this is *our* car; that is *your* car); if you mean *you are*, use *you're* (remember that the apostrophe means the *a* has been omitted).

  If you're in the sun in Florida, be sure to put sunscreen on your nose.

Chapter 2

Punctuation

In elementary school, you learned that each punctuation mark sends a certain message. By applying the "code" of punctuation and capitalization properly, your readers are able to understand your words in the way you intended. However, when readers and writers don't use the same format—the same code—for applying capital letters and punctuation marks, confusion often results. Using the rules of the code enables you and your readers to understand the same things. Take a look at the following:

> *when the envelope arrived i opened it and screamed this is it i yelled in a voice that was loud enough to wake up the whole neighborhood running up from the basement my husband asked whats wrong nothings wrong i hastened to reply weve just become the latest winners in the state sweepstakes now well have enough money to go on that vacation weve dreamed about*

At this point you've probably given up trying to decipher what's being said. Obviously, the words are jumbled together without any capitalization or punctuation, so reading them requires both time and trouble on your part. However, if the story is rewritten and uses appropriate capital letters and punctuation marks, then it's a snap to read.

When the envelope arrived, I opened it and screamed. "This is it!" I yelled in a voice that was loud enough to wake up the whole neighborhood.

Running up from the basement, my husband asked, "What's wrong?"

"Nothing's wrong," I hastened to reply. "We've just become the latest winners in the state sweepstakes. Now we'll have enough money to go on that vacation we've dreamed about."

Much better, wouldn't you say? The same words are used, but now you can easily read and understand the story because capital letters and punctuation marks have been correctly inserted.

END PUNCTUATION

The End of the Sentence Road

Let's begin at the end—of sentences, that is. Three marks signal that a sentence is over: a period, a question mark, and an exclamation point.

THE PERIOD

A period is most often used to signal the end of a sentence that states a fact or one that gives a command or makes a request. For example:

The majority of the viewers stopped watching the program after the format was changed.

Hand me the pen that rolled near you.

If a sentence reports a fact that contains a question, a period should be used at the end. Look at this sentence:

I wondered if you could join me tonight for a night on the town.

The end punctuation should be a period because the sentence as a whole states a fact (that I'm wondering something) rather than asks a question.

Grammar Facts

You shouldn't put a space between the last letter of the sentence and the end mark, but this mistake is commonly made. Other languages do insert a space, but in English the end mark comes immediately after the final word.

If your declarative or imperative sentence ends with an abbreviation that takes a period, don't put an additional period at the end. Write:

I'll be at your apartment to pick you up at 8 P.M.
not
I'll be at your apartment to pick you up at 8 P.M..

Periods are also used in abbreviations, such as *Dr., Ms., Rev., i.e.,* and *et al.*

QUESTION MARKS

Question marks go at the end of direct questions and sentences that end in questions. But you knew that, didn't you? Couldn't that information have been left out? You get the picture, don't you? Surely the point has sunk in by now, hasn't it?

A question mark is also used to show that there's doubt or uncertainty about something written in a sentence, such as a name, a date, or a word. In birth and death dates, such as (?–1565), the question mark means the birth date hasn't been verified. Look at this example:

The police are searching for Richard-O (?) in connection with the crime.

Here, the question mark means that the author is uncertain about the person's name. But look at this example:

Paul said he would donate five thousand dollars (?) to the charity.

The question mark means that the author is unsure about the exact amount of the donation.

Watch to see if a question mark is part of a title. If it is, be sure to include it in any punctuation that goes with the title:

I won't watch that new television program Can You Believe It?

Grammar Facts

Remember, question marks go inside quotation marks if the quoted material forms a question. Otherwise, question marks go outside quotation marks. Notice the difference in these examples:

Brendan asked, "Where in the world are those reports?"
Did Brendan say, "I thought I gave you the reports"?

If you have a series of questions that aren't complete sentences, a question mark should be included after each fragment:

Can you believe that it's ten below zero? or that it's snowing? or that my electricity has gone off? or that the telephone has gone out?

EXCLAMATION POINTS

Exclamation points (exclamation marks) are used to express strong feelings! There's quite a difference between these two sentences:

Out of the blue, Marsha called Morris last night.
Out of the blue, Marsha called Morris last night!

The second sentence tells readers that there was something extraordinary about the fact that Marsha called Morris.

In formal writing, don't use exclamation points (unless, of course, you're quoting a source or citing a title—or working for a tabloid magazine). In informal writing, you might include exclamation points after information that you find to be remarkable or information that you're excited about:

Paul said that he would donate five thousand dollars (!) to the charity.

or

Paul said that he would donate five thousand dollars to the charity!

Check to see if an exclamation point is part of a title. If it is, be sure to include it:

I won't watch that new television program I Can't Believe It!

Grammar Facts

Only in informal writing should you use more than one question mark or exclamation mark:

Is this picture of our former roommate on Instagram for real????

or

I can't believe that our former roommate's Instagram has almost a million followers!!!

QUOTATION MARKS

When the Words Are Not Your Own

Use quotation marks (" ") at the beginning and ending of words, phrases, or sentences to show which words belong to you (the writer) and which belong to someone else.

The term *double quotes* is synonymous with *quotation marks*. You'll learn about single quotes (' ') later.

The most common use of quotation marks is to show readers the exact words a person said, in the exact order the person spoke them. This is called a direct quotation. Note the difference in these sentences:

Direct Quotation
Amber Posey said, "Give me the book."

Indirect Quotation
Amber Posey said to give her the book.

Direct Quotation
Carla Fenwick replied, "I don't have the book."

Indirect Quotation
Carla Fenwick replied she didn't have the book.

The same meaning is conveyed either way, but the quotation marks tell readers the words are stated exactly as they were spoken.

One of the most common mistakes that is made with quotation marks is to use them immediately after a word such as *said* or *asked*. Quotation marks are used *correctly* in sentences like these:

Harry asked, "Anna, will you pass me the butter?"
Anna said, "We don't have any butter."

The mistake comes in sentences that are indirect quotations (that is, the words after *said*, *asked*, and so on aren't the exact words, in the exact order, that the speaker used).

Consider this sentence, which gives the same information about Harry and Anna:

Harry asked if Anna would pass him the butter.

The mistake often made is to punctuate that sentence this way:

Harry asked, "If Anna would pass him the butter."

But the words inside the quotation marks aren't the exact words, in the exact order, that Harry used. Since these aren't the exact words, quotation marks can't be used.

Grammar Facts

The quotation mark can be traced back to the second century when a librarian named Aristarchus created the symbol while editing the works in the Library of Alexandria. He placed "diples" alongside text that was noteworthy. Later in the seventh century the mark would be used in the books of churchmen to separate the citations from Sacred Scripture from their own.

QUOTATION GUIDELINES

Guideline 1

Every time you change speakers, indent and start a new paragraph, even if the person quoted is just saying one word. This is the signal for readers to keep straight who's saying what. Take a look at this sequence:

When the telephone rang, Nick picked up the receiver and said, "Hello." Nora screamed into her end of the phone, "Who is this?" "Nick." "Nick who?" "Well, who is this?" "You know darned well who this is. You've sure called me often enough to know the sound of my voice!" "Huh?" "That's right. I'm hopping mad, and you know why."

Are you confused yet? Written that way, readers can't follow who's saying what. The dialogue should start a new paragraph each time the speaker changes. Then readers can identify the speaker. This is the way the passage should be written:

When the telephone rang, Nick picked up the receiver and said, "Hello."

　　Nora screamed into her end of the phone, "Who is this?"
　　"Nick."
　　"Nick who?"
　　"Well, who is this?"
　　"You know darned well who this is. You've sure called me often enough to know the sound of my voice!"
　　"Huh?"
　　"That's right. I'm hopping mad, and you know why."

Guideline 2

If you're quoting more than one sentence from the same source (a person or a manuscript), put the closing quotation marks at the end of the speaker's last sentence of that paragraph *only*, not at the end of each sentence. This helps readers know that the same person is speaking. For example:

At the diner, Leslie said, "I'll start with a cup of coffee and a large orange juice. Then I want scrambled eggs, bacon, and toast for breakfast. May I get home fries with that?"

No quotation marks come after *juice* or *breakfast*. That tells readers that Leslie hasn't finished speaking.

Guideline 3

If you're quoting more than one paragraph from the same source (a person or a manuscript), put beginning quotation marks at the start of each paragraph of your quote and closing quotation marks *only* at the end of the last paragraph. This lets readers know that the words come from the same source, without any interruption. Take a look at this example:

> *The ransom letter read:*
>
> *"We'll expect to receive the ransom money by this afternoon. You can get it from your Grandfather Moss. We know he's loaded.*
> *"Tell him not to try any funny stuff. We want the money in unmarked bills, and we don't want any police involved."*

At the end of the first paragraph the word *loaded* isn't followed by quotation marks, and quotation marks are placed at the beginning and end of the second paragraph. This tells readers that the same person is speaking or the same source is being quoted. The closing quotation marks designate when the quotation ends.

Guideline 4

Use quotation marks to enclose the titles of short works (short poems, short stories, titles of articles from magazines or newspapers, essays, chapters of books, songs, and episodes of television or radio programs):

> *To get the information for my book, I'm consulting a chapter called "The Art of Detection" from the book* How Mysteries Are Written.

> *Mary Lynn and Pat decided their favorite song is "Love Letters," from the CD* ABC and XYZ of Love.

Guideline 5

If you're using slang, technical terms, or other expressions outside their normal usage, enclose the words or phrases in quotation marks (alternately, you may put the words or phrases in italics):

My grandmother didn't know if it was a compliment or an insult when I described my best friend as being "phat."

In computer discussion groups, what does "start a new thread" mean?

Using the quotation marks lets readers know which particular words or phrases you're emphasizing.

Guideline 6

Remember that periods and commas go *inside* closing quotation marks; colons and semicolons go *outside* closing quotation marks. If you examine a work closely, you'll see that following this rule doesn't really look right (and it isn't adhered to in British English), but it's the correct punctuation in the United States. Look at this sentence:

I was reading the short story "Scared Out of My Wits," but I fell asleep in spite of myself.

See the comma after *Wits* and before the closing quotation marks? The actual title of the story is "Scared Out of My Wits" (there's no comma in the title). However, the sentence continues and demands a comma, so U.S. English requires a comma to be placed *inside* the closing quotation marks. Now look at this sentence:

I was reading the short story "Scared Out of My Wits"; I didn't find it to be scary at all.

The semicolon is *outside* the closing quotation marks after *Wits*.

Guideline 7

Deciding on placement of the two other end marks of punctuation—the question mark and the exclamation mark—is tricky: These go either *inside* or *outside* the closing marks, depending on what's being quoted. Take, for instance, a question mark. It goes *inside* the closing quotation if what is being quoted is a question:

Jica said, "Did you fall asleep reading the story?"

The words that Jica said form the question, so the question mark goes *inside* the closing quotation mark to show readers what she said. Look at this example:

Pat shouted, "I hope you know what you're doing!"

Again, the words that Pat said form the exclamation, so the exclamation mark goes inside the closing quotation marks. Now take a look at this example:

Did Martha say, "You must have fallen asleep"?

Now the words that Martha said ("You must have fallen asleep") don't form a question; the sentence as a whole does. The question mark goes outside the closing quotation marks to show readers that.

Martha actually said, "You must be right"!

Again, the words that Martha said don't form an exclamation; the sentence as a whole does (probably expressing surprise). The exclamation mark goes *outside* the closing quotation marks to show readers that.

What do you do when both the sentence as a whole *and* the words being quoted form a question or an exclamation? Use only *one* end mark (question mark or exclamation mark) and put it *inside* the closing quotation marks. Look at this example:

Did I hear Martha say, "Who called this afternoon?"

QUOTES WITHIN QUOTES

In the United States, single quotation marks are used for a quotation within a quotation:

"Mark Lester said, 'I'll be fine,' but then he collapsed," cried Marrin Wright.

"I'm reading the story 'Plaid Blazers and Other Mysteries,'" said Tara Hoggard.

Do you see that what Mark said ("I'll be fine") and the name of the short story ("Plaid Blazers and Other Mysteries") would normally be enclosed with double quotation marks? But since these phrases come inside material that's already in double marks, you show readers where the quotation (or title) begins by using a single quotation mark.

When not to use quotation marks with quotes: If you're using the writing guidelines from the Modern Language Association (MLA) or the American Psychological Association (APA), keep in mind that these groups have specific rules for block quotations (passages of a certain length). In spite of the fact that you're quoting, you don't use quotation marks. You do, however, have a definite format for letting readers know that the material you're citing is verbatim from the original text. Consult the specific guidelines for each group to see how to format this material.

THE APOSTROPHE

Misunderstood Mark

There is probably no more misused mark of punctuation than the apostrophe. This tricky little punctuation mark creates more havoc and incorrect grammar than any other. Unlike many other marks of punctuation, apostrophes are often overused by many people. You'll often see them popping up in advertisements and signs where they have no need to be. This misplacement often leads to a serious corruption of the original sentence and can change the meaning the writer intended to convey, which is why it is crucial that you understand the correct placement and usage of this mark.

Because people become confused about the purpose of apostrophes, they end up using them in all sorts of creative ways. Perhaps you've done so yourself. If so, take heart, because you're certainly not alone. You can walk into almost any store and see signs like the following that feature the incorrect use of the apostrophe:

Special price's this week!
Rent two movie's today!
Five can's for $4.00!

In these examples, none of the words that have an apostrophe needs one. Each is a simple plural, and you almost never need to use an apostrophe to denote a plural. Using an apostrophe correctly doesn't have to be difficult.

There are three basic situations in which an apostrophe would be the correct choice:

1. Contractions
2. Possession
3. Forming a plural (rare)

That's it. Funny how often this mark is used when it really only has a limited number of circumstances that truly need it. Let's dive deeper into when you will need the apostrophe in the following sections. We'll start with the easiest use of the apostrophe, the contraction.

CONTRACTIONS

An apostrophe often indicates that at least one letter has been omitted from a word, and the word that's formed is called a contraction. For example, the contraction *don't* stands for *do not*; the *o* in *not* has been omitted. *I'll* is a short form of *I will*; in this case the *wi* of *will* has been omitted. Here are some examples of the most common contractions:

- *are not* becomes *aren't*
- *cannot* becomes *can't*
- *could not* becomes *couldn't*
- *did not* becomes *didn't*
- *does not* becomes *doesn't*
- *do not* becomes *don't*
- *had not* becomes *hadn't*
- *has not* becomes *hasn't*
- *have not* becomes *haven't*
- *he had, he would* becomes *he'd*
- *he will, he shall* becomes *he'll*
- *he is, he has* becomes *he's*
- *I had, I would* becomes *I'd*
- *I will, I shall* becomes *I'll*
- *I am* becomes *I'm*
- *I have* becomes *I've*
- *is not* becomes *isn't*
- *let us* becomes *let's*

- *might not* becomes *mightn't*
- *must not* becomes *mustn't*
- *shall not* becomes *shan't*
- *she had, she would* becomes *she'd*
- *she will, she shall* becomes *she'll*
- *she is, she has* becomes *she's*
- *should not* becomes *shouldn't*
- *that is, that has* becomes *that's*
- *there is, there has* becomes *there's*
- *they had, they would* becomes *they'd*
- *they will, they shall* becomes *they'll*
- *they are* becomes *they're*
- *they have* becomes *they've*
- *we had, we would* becomes *we'd*
- *we are* becomes *we're*
- *we have* becomes *we've*
- *were not* becomes *weren't*
- *what will, what shall* becomes *what'll*
- *what are* becomes *what're*
- *what is, what has* becomes *what's*
- *what have* becomes *what've*
- *where is, where has* becomes *where's*
- *who had, who would* becomes *who's*
- *who will, who shall* becomes *who'll*
- *who are* becomes *who're*
- *who is, who has* becomes *who's*
- *who have* becomes *who've*
- *will not* becomes *won't*
- *would not* becomes *wouldn't*
- *you had, you would* becomes *you'd*
- *you will, you shall* becomes *you'll*
- *you are* becomes *you're*
- *you have* becomes *you've*

Additionally, sometimes authors will use apostrophes in contractions to help readers understand dialect. For instance, an author might write, "Alice is goin' swimmin' today." Readers understand that the final -gs are omitted from *going* and *swimming*, and that the author is trying to duplicate the type of speech (the dialect) a character uses.

POSSESSION

Before using an apostrophe to show possession, first make sure the phrase you're questioning actually denotes possession and isn't simply a plural. For instance, in the phrase *the babies' rattles*, the babies possess rattles (so an apostrophe indicates this to readers); however, in the phrase *the babies in their cribs*, the babies aren't possessing anything and an apostrophe isn't needed.

Grammar Facts

One of the most common mistakes with apostrophes comes with possessive pronouns (*its, yours, his, hers, theirs, ours, whose*). Remember that the only one of these words that ever takes an apostrophe is *its*, and that happens only when the word means *it is*.

Here are some guidelines to help you make sense of it all.

Guideline 1

If a singular noun doesn't end in -s, its possessive ends in -'s. Say what? Take a look at this sentence:

The cars engine was still running.

The word *cars* needs an apostrophe to indicate possession, but where does the apostrophe go?

Use this mental trick: Take the word that needs the apostrophe (*cars*) and the word that it's talking about (*engine*) and mentally turn the two words around so that the word you're wondering about is the object of a preposition. (This rule may be easier for you to understand this way: Turn the words around so that they form a phrase. Usually the phrase will use *of*, *from*, or *belonging to*.)

When you change *cars engine* around, you come up with *engine of the car*. Now look at the word *car*. *Car* is singular and doesn't end in -*s*, so the original should be punctuated -'*s*. You should have:

The car's engine was still running.

Try the trick again with this sentence:

Donna Moores wallet was lying on the seat.

Mentally turn Donna Moores wallet around so that you have the wallet of (belonging to) Donna Moore.

After you've turned it around, you have the words *Donna Moore*, which is singular (in spite of being two words) and doesn't end in -*s*. That lets you know that you need to use -'*s*. The sentence should be punctuated this way:

Donna Moore's wallet was lying on the seat.

Guideline 2

When you have plural nouns that end in -*s* (and most do), add an apostrophe after the final -*s*. This tells readers that you're talking about several people, places, or things. The same mental trick of turning the two words into a phrase applies.

This sentence talks about two girls who had been reported missing:

The girls coats were found at the bus station.

Now just apply the trick. Take the phrase *girls coats*, and turn it around so that you have *coats of (belonging to) the girls.*

When you've turned the phrase around this time, the word *girls* ends in -*s*. This lets you know that you should add an apostrophe after the -*s* in *girls*, so the sentence is punctuated this way:

The girls' coats were found at the bus station.

Although most English plurals end in -*s* or -*es*, our language has a number of exceptions (and didn't you know there would be?), such as *children, women,* and *deer.* If a plural doesn't end in -*s*, the possessive is formed with an -*'s* (that is, treat it as if it were singular).

Again, the turnaround trick applies. Take the sentence:

The childrens coats were covered with mud.

Mentally turn *childrens coats* into the phrase *coats of the children.* Since *children* doesn't end in -*s*, its possessive would be -*'s*; so the correct punctuation would be:

The children's coats were covered with mud.

So far, so good? You have just one tricky part left to consider. It concerns singular words that end in -*s*. Two ways of punctuating these words are common. Guideline 3 is used more often than Guideline 4, but many people find that Guideline 4 is easier to grasp.

Guideline 3

If a singular word ends in -*s*, form its possessive by adding -*'s* (except in situations in which pronunciation would be difficult, such as *Moses* or *Achilles*). Look at this sentence:

Julie Jones information was invaluable in locating the missing girls.

Applying the turnaround trick would make the phrase that needs the apostrophe read this way: *information from Julie Jones.*

Guideline 3 would tell you that, since *Jones* is singular and ends in -*s*, you'd form the possessive by adding -*'s*. Therefore, the sentence would be punctuated this way:

Julie Jones's information was invaluable in locating the missing girls.

However, you may be told to use another rule:

Guideline 4

If a singular word ends in -*s*, form its possessive by adding an apostrophe after the -*s*. In this case, the sentence would be written this way:

Julie Jones' information was invaluable in locating the missing girls.

If using Guideline 4 is okay with your teacher or employer, then you have to remember only two rules about placing the apostrophe in possessives:

1. After you mentally turn the phrase around, if the word in question doesn't end in -*s*, add -*'s*.
2. After you mentally turn the phrase around, if the word in question ends in -*s*, add an apostrophe after the -*s*.

Joint versus Individual Possession

One use of apostrophes shows readers whether the people you're talking about possess (own) something jointly or individually. Take a look at this sentence:

Jim and Allisons cars were stolen.

The question is, did Jim and Allison own the cars together or separately? If, say, Jim and Allison were a married couple and they had the misfortune of having two of their cars stolen, then the sentence would be punctuated this way:

Jim and Allison's cars were stolen.

The possessive comes after the last person's name *only*. This usage tells readers that Jim and Allison had joint ownership of the cars.

But maybe Jim and Allison were neighbors, and a rash of car thefts had taken place on their block. The sentence would then be punctuated this way:

Jim's and Allison's cars were stolen.

The possessive comes after *both* names. This tells readers that Jim and Allison had separate ownership of the cars.

FORMING PLURALS

Take another look at the store signs mentioned at the beginning of this section that incorrectly used an apostrophe:

Special price's this week!
Rent two movie's today!
Five can's for $4.00!

The words that have apostrophes are just plain plurals; they don't show ownership in any way and so don't need apostrophes. (If you're unsure about whether you should use an apostrophe, ask yourself if the word in question owns or possesses anything.)

Also, if you have proverbial expressions that involve individual letters or combinations of letters, use apostrophes to show their plurals.

Dot your i's and cross your t's.

In these examples, some style academic or company guides dictate that you shouldn't italicize the letter you're making plural; other guides take the opposite view. Be sure to consult the guide suggested by your instructor or company.

Another time that you should use an apostrophe to form a plural is if your reader would be confused by reading an -s alone (for instance, when an -s is added to an individual letter or letter combination or to numbers used as nouns).

s's (instead of ss)
Write 7's (instead of 7s) *in the graph.*

Capital letters used as words, however, just take an -s without an apostrophe for their plural form:

My grandfather only learned the three Rs when he attended school.

Susie was happy she received all As on her report card.

THE COMMA

The Perfect Pause

Commas are used more frequently than any other punctuation mark. Like all other punctuation marks, use a comma to keep your readers from being confused. When readers see a comma, they know a slight pause comes at that place in the sentence, and they can tell how particular words or phrases relate to other parts of the sentence. Take a look at this sentence:

Will you call Mary Alice Lee and Jason or should I?

What's being said here? This sentence has entirely different meanings, depending on how commas are placed in it.

Will you call Mary, Alice, Lee, and Jason, or should I?
Will you call Mary Alice, Lee, and Jason, or should I?
Will you call Mary, Alice Lee, and Jason, or should I?

USING COMMAS WITH A SERIES

If you have a series of items, use a comma to separate the items. Take a look at this sentence:

The convertible 2008 Ford and Chevy pickup were involved in a wreck.

How many vehicles were involved? With the following punctuation, you'd see that three vehicles were involved.

The convertible, 2008 Ford, and Chevy pickup...

However, this punctuation shows that only two vehicles were involved.

The convertible 2008 Ford and Chevy pickup . . .

Use a comma between two or more adjectives (words that explain or describe or give more information about a noun or pronoun) that modify a noun (the name of a person, place, thing, or idea):

The man in the torn, tattered jacket moved quickly through the crowded, unlit street.

If the first adjective modifies the idea expressed by the combination of subsequent adjectives and the noun, then you don't need commas. Look at this sentence:

Many countries don't have stable central governments.

Since *central governments* would be considered a single unit, you don't need to separate it from the adjective modifying it (*stable*) with a comma.

If you're using *and, or,* or *nor* to connect all the items in the series, don't use commas:

The flag is red and white and blue.
The flag might be red or white or blue.
The flag is neither red nor white nor blue.

COMMAS WITH COMPOUND SENTENCES

If you have two independent clauses (that is, two thoughts that could stand alone as sentences) and they're joined by *but, or, yet, so, for, and*, or *nor* (use the mnemonic *boysfan* to help you remember), join them with a comma:

> *It was more than three hours past lunchtime, and everybody was grumbling about being hungry.*

The exception: You may eliminate the comma if the two independent clauses are short and if the sentence would still be clear without the comma. For example:

> *We filled up with gas and we went on our way.*

If you have a simple sentence with a compound verb, don't put a comma between the verbs:

> *I wanted to get some rest [no comma] but needed to get more work done.*

Grammar Facts

Some style guides mandate that the final two items in a series (also referred to as the "serial comma," "Harvard comma," or "Oxford comma") always be separated by commas; other guides dictate that it be eliminated, except in cases where the meaning would be misconstrued without it. You should find out which style your instructor or company prefers.

Commas with Quoted Material

If a quoted sentence is interrupted by words such as *he said* or *she replied*, use commas in this way:

> *"For this contest," he said, "you need three pencils and two pieces of paper."*

The first comma goes before the closing quotation mark and the second comma goes before the beginning quotation mark.

If the words being quoted make up a question or an exclamation, don't include a comma:

"Put that down right now!" Barry cried.

Grammar Facts

Avoid using a comma with words that are generally thought of as pairs—even if they're in a series. For instance, you'd write:

I ate an apple, an orange, and peanut butter and jelly every day while I was in grade school.

Since peanut butter and jelly are often though of as one food, don't put a comma after *butter*.

MORE USES FOR COMMAS

Use commas to set apart clauses (groups of words that have a subject and a predicate), participial phrases (see Chapter 8), and appositives (words or phrases that give information about a noun or pronoun) that aren't necessary to the meaning of the sentence.

Take a look at this sentence:

The handsome man over there, the only one who works in the deli at Sam's Supermarket, has black hair and brown eyes.

If you took out the clause *the only one who works in the deli at Sam's Supermarket*, you'd still have the same essential parts of the sentence. You don't need to know where the man works in order to learn his hair and eye color. (The nonessential part of this sentence is called a nonrestrictive clause. See Chapter 8 for more information.) Here's another way of looking at it: If you can take out the part in question (the part you're questioning for commas) and the sentence still makes sense, then you should use the commas. Now look:

The only man who works in the deli at Sam's Supermarket was arrested for stealing four grapes and five apples.

In this case, if you removed *who works in the deli at Sam's Supermarket,* you'd have *The only man was arrested for stealing four grapes and five apples.* That isn't the meaning of the original sentence. Remember: If you need the extra words for the meaning, you don't need the commas.

Grammar Facts

A mistake that seems to be cropping up more and more is using a comma to separate a verb from its subject (As in "The flour, had been infested with bugs"). The comma after *flour* should be eliminated.

Commas are also used after introductory words such as exclamations, common expressions, and names used in direct address that aren't necessary for the meaning of a sentence. If you have words that begin a sentence and you could understand the sentence without them, use a comma to separate them from the rest of the sentence. For example:

Why, don't you look nice tonight!
Now, what was I supposed to remember?
If you must know, I have been dyeing my hair for the past ten years.

A comma is also used before these same types of words and phrases when they appear at the end of a sentence, as long as they're not necessary for the meaning:

Don't you think that new song really rocks, Madison?
You're not going to the party, are you?
Call me back at your convenience, if you please.

Use commas around words that interrupt a sentence (these words are called parenthetical expressions), as long as the words aren't necessary for the meaning:

The answer to the next question, Paula, can be found on page thirty-six.

This textbook, unlike the one I had before, is written in a style I can understand.

Use a comma after an introductory verbal (a verbal is a participle, gerund, or infinitive) or verbal phrase:
Weeping at the sight of the destruction, the news reporter broke down on camera.

To try to regain her composure, Allison took several deep breaths.

Use a comma after an introductory adverb clause. (An adverb clause is a group of words that has a subject and a verb, and describes a verb, adjective, or other adverb.) For example:

Because Reagan didn't stop at the red light, she got a ticket.

If Grant comes in town tonight, the whole family is going to get together for a picnic.

USING COMMAS IN ADDRESSES

When writing out a mailing address as text (not on separate lines), put a comma between the person's last name and the start of the street address, then after the street address, then between the city and the state. Don't put a comma between the state and the zip code. For example:

Please remit the payment to Cooper Bartlett, 4238 Old Highway 41 North, Nicholasville, KY 42309.

If you're putting address information on separate lines, use a comma only between the city and state:

Cooper Bartlett
4238 Old Highway 41 North
Nicholasville, KY 42309.

If you mention a city and state in text, put commas around the state:

I have to visit Clinton, Iowa, on my next sales trip.

The same is true if you mention a city and country; put commas around the country.

USING COMMAS IN DATES

Put a comma after the day of the week (if you've stated it), the day of the month, and the year (if the sentence continues):

John Abbott will meet you on Friday, February 22, 2008, at half past seven.

If you're writing only the day and month or the month and year, no comma is necessary:

John Abbott will meet you on February 22.
John Abbott will meet you in February 2008.

USING COMMAS IN LETTERS

Put a comma after the greeting (salutation) of all friendly letters and the closing of all letters:

Dear Aunt Helen,
Sincerely,

USING COMMAS WITH TITLES OR DEGREES

If a person's title or degree follows his or her name, put commas after or around it:

Please call Robert Householder, PhD, at your convenience.
The deposition was given by Edward Shuttleworth, MD.

USING COMMAS WITH LONG NUMBERS

Using commas helps readers understand long numbers more easily. If, for instance, you read the number 1376993, you'd have to stop, count the numbers, and then group them in threes before you could understand the number. Using commas to divide the numbers makes for quicker interpretation:

Is it my imagination, or does this book list 1,376,993 rules for commas?

Chapter 3

Colons, Semicolons, Dashes, and More

A few punctuation marks—in particular, colons and semicolons, hyphens and dashes, and parentheses and brackets—are closely linked in appearance, if not in function. This can cause confusion for the writer—and has even been known to strike fear into the heart of some. But fear not! This chapter will clear up any ambiguity surrounding these punctuation pairs and will give you the tools you need to be able to use them with confidence.

THE COLON

Something Is Coming . . .

Colons are used to introduce particular information. An important thing to remember about colons is that they must follow a complete sentence. You should never use a colon after a sentence fragment. The colon will signal that what follows it is directly related to the previous sentence, but that previous sentence should be able to stand on its own if the colon was not there. For example,

Kate has two favorite animals: dogs and rabbits.

The sentence before the colon, *Kate has two favorite animals,* could stand on its own and doesn't necessarily need what follows the colon so this use of a colon is correct. However,

Kate's two favorite animals are: cats and rabbits.

The phrase, *Kate's favorite animals are,* is a sentence fragment and cannot stand on its own so this sentence would be an improper use of a colon.

Here are some other examples of proper colon use:

My feet are soaking wet: I forgot my rain boots.
Dan knows how to accomplish his goal: one step at at time.
The test was very difficult: it covered new material.

One of the most common uses of a colon is to signal to readers that a list will follow:

On the camping trip, please bring the following: a flashlight, a sleeping bag, two boxes of matches, and food for six meals.

You can also use a colon to explain or give more information about what has come before it in a sentence:

I have a number of complaints against the tenant: damaged plaster, dog-stained carpet in every room, and three months of unpaid rent.

Also, in formal papers, a colon usually precedes a lengthy quotation:

In his Gettysburg Address, Abraham Lincoln stated: Four score and seven years ago, our forefathers brought forth on this continent a new nation, conceived in liberty and dedicated to the proposition that all men are created equal.

Grammar Facts

If you have a list that is the object of a verb or of a preposition, you don't need a colon:

On the camping trip, please bring a flashlight, a sleeping bag, two boxes of matches, and food for six meals. (The list is the object of the verb *bring*.)

On the camping trip, please bring your supplies to Tom, Sally, Mykela, or Fernando. (The list is the object of the preposition *to*.)

To be on the safe side, use an expression such as *the following* or *as follows* before a colon.

To determine what is meant by "lengthy," consult the style guide designated by your instructor or employer.

Here are other times to use a colon:

- In the greeting of a business letter

  To Whom It May Concern:

- Between the hour and minutes in time

  a meeting at 4:15 P.M.

- In dividing a title from its subtitle

  My Favorite Punctuation Marks: Why I Love Colons

- In naming a chapter and verse of the Bible

  Genesis 2:10

- In naming the volume and number of a magazine

  Time 41:14

- In citing the volume and page number of a magazine

  U.S. News and World Report 166: 31

- Between the city and the publisher in a bibliographical entry

  London: Covent Garden Press

THE SEMICOLON

Pause for Effect

Semicolons signal a pause greater than one indicated by a comma but less than one indicated by a period. The most common use for a semicolon is joining two complete thoughts (independent clauses) into one sentence.

Look at the following sentences:

The bank teller determined the bill was counterfeit. No serial number was on it.

Each of these sentences stands alone, but they could be joined by using a semicolon:

The bank teller determined the bill was counterfeit; no serial number was on it.

Grammar Facts

In English, many transitional words and phrases are commonly used. Here are a few of them: *first*, *second*, *third*, *next*, *finally*, *then*, *moreover*, *likewise*, and *similarly*.

Often semicolons are used with conjunctive adverbs and other transitional words or phrases, such as *on the other hand* or *therefore*. In this case, be sure that you put the semicolon at the point where the two thoughts are separated. For example:

- **Right:** There is more to this case than meets the eye; however, you'll have to wait to read about it in the newspapers.

- **Wrong:** There is more to this case than meets the eye, you'll; however, have to read about it in the newspapers.

Semicolons are sometimes used at the end of bulleted or numbered lists, depending on the style and the sentence construction. (Sometimes commas or periods are used, and sometimes there's no punctuation at all.) A list may appear like this:

In order to receive your award, you must do the following:
*   1. verify that you have been a member for at least three years;*
*   2. submit copies of civic or charitable work done in the name of the club;*
*   3. have at least three letters of recommendation.*

Now it's time to break a rule about semicolons. Sometimes you use a semicolon when a comma might seem to be the correct punctuation mark. Look at this sentence:

The manhunt took place in Los Angeles, Nashville, Indiana, Stratford, Connecticut, Enid, Oklahoma, Dallas, and Olympia.

Commas came after the name of each city and each state, as the rule on commas says they should. However, readers will probably be confused about the true meaning of the sentence. Consider that a semicolon is a "notch above" a comma. By substituting a semicolon in places where you'd ordinarily use a comma, you make the material clearer for readers by showing which cities go with which states. Look at how the sentence should be punctuated:

The manhunt took place in Los Angeles; Nashville, Indiana; Stratford, Connecticut; Enid, Oklahoma; Dallas; and Olympia.

Reading the sentence with semicolons used in this way, readers can tell that the manhunt took place in Nashville, Indiana, as opposed to Nashville, Tennessee. Also, readers can identify that Enid is located in Oklahoma.

WHEN NOT TO USE SEMICOLONS

Semicolons won't work if the two thoughts aren't on the same playing field (that is, if they're not logically connected). Look at these two sentences:

The teller wore a blue suit. The police were called immediately.

Although both are sentences, they have no logical link. If a semicolon were used between these two sentences, readers would be scratching their heads, thinking they were missing something.

Semicolons also won't work if one of the thoughts isn't a complete sentence. Look at this example:

The police were called immediately; screeching through the streets.

The first part of the sentence is a complete thought (*the police were called immediately*), but the second part isn't (*screeching through the streets*).

THE HYPHEN, DASH, AND SLASH
Dividing Words and Thoughts

Hyphens and dashes are another tricky punctuation pair. A hyphen is a short horizontal line (next to a zero on a keyboard); a dash is longer. But the differences between them go much deeper than just a few fractions of an inch.

The most common use of the hyphen is to divide words at the ends of lines. It's important to remember that you may divide words only between syllables. Why is this important, you ask? Read the following lines:

Sarah was unhappy with her oldest child, her nineteen-year-old da-ughter Lindsay. Lindsay was still relying on her mother to get her up wh-en the alarm clock rang in the mornings, to see that her various deadli-nes for typing papers for school were met, to take her side in the cons-tant squabbles with her boyfriend, Harry.

See how difficult this is to read? That's because you've learned to read in syllables. When words aren't divided correctly, readers have to go back to the previous line and put the syllables together, and that's confusing and time-consuming.

The text should read:

Sarah was unhappy with her oldest child, her nineteen-year-old daughter Lindsay. Lindsay was still relying on her mother to get her up when the alarm clock rang in the mornings, to see that her various dead-lines for typing papers for school were met, to take her side in the con-stant squabbles with her boyfriend, Harry.

If you're not sure where syllables occur, consult a dictionary. In addition, most word processing software contains automatic hyphenation tools you may use. Since you may divide a word only between its syllables, one-syllable words may not be divided.

No matter where the words are divided, be careful to leave more than one letter at the end of a line (or more than two at the beginning of a line) so that readers' eyes can adjust quickly.

You wouldn't write:

Beth wondered if the employment agency would call her back a-gain for another interview.

Nor would you write:

Beth killed her chances for another interview when she contact-ed the company president by telephone.

You should also avoid hyphenating acronyms (such as UNESCO or NAACP), numerals (such as 1,200 or 692), and contractions (such as haven't, didn't, couldn't). Also, some style guides say that proper nouns (those that are capitalized) shouldn't be hyphenated.

Also try to avoid dividing an Internet or email address. Since these addresses often contain hyphens as part of the address, inserting an extra hyphen would certainly confuse readers. If angle brackets aren't used, extending the address to the second line without any extra punctuation would make the address clear for your reader. You should do that this way:

When I tried to order, I was directed to this site: www.anglosaxon.com/rebates/year/1066.

Hyphens with Compound Adjectives

When a compound adjective (two or more adjectives that go together to form one thought or image) precedes the noun it modifies, it should be hyphenated. Look at these sentences:

Charles Dickens was a nineteenth-century writer.

In this case, *nineteenth-century* is an adjective (it modifies the noun *writer*), and so it's hyphenated. Notice the difference:

Charles Dickens was a writer who lived in the nineteenth century.

Here, *nineteenth century* is a noun, so it's not hyphenated.

Use a hyphen to join adjectives only if together they form the image. If they're separate words describing a noun (as *big, bulky package*), then don't use a hyphen. Take a look at this example:

loyal, long-time friend

Long and *time* go together to form the image that describes the friend, so they're hyphenated. If the hyphen weren't there, then readers would see *long time friend* and would wonder what a *long friend* was or what a *time friend* was.

Hyphens for Numbers

Another common use of the hyphen comes when numbers are written as words instead of numerals. You probably do this already, but the rule says to hyphenate numbers from twenty-one to ninety-nine. If you look at words printed without a hyphen (e.g., sixtyfour, eightyseven), you see that they're difficult to read. Using hyphens makes reading easier.

Hyphens for Clarification

Sometimes you should use a hyphen to clarify the meaning of your sentence. For instance, look at this example:

My favorite sports star resigned!

Should you be elated or upset? The way the sentence is punctuated now, the star will no longer play; his or her fans will be upset. If, however, the writer intended to get across that the star had signed another contract, the sentence should contain a hyphen and be written this way:

My favorite sports star re-signed!

Now you understand the writer's intent. Not many words have this idiosyncrasy (*recreation* and *recollect* are two others), but be careful of those that do.

Grammar Facts

If a modifier before a noun is the word *very* or is an adverb that ends in *-ly*, you don't need a hyphen. You should write:

a very condescending attitude
a strictly guarded secret
a very little amount of money
the highly publicized meeting

THE DASH

A dash provides a window for some informality in writing, allowing the writer to introduce an abrupt change in thought or tone. Look at this sentence:

The odometer just reached thirty thousand miles, so it's time to call the garage for—oops! I just passed the street where we were supposed to turn.

The dash tells readers that a sudden idea interrupted the speaker's original thought.

Use a dash to give emphasis to something that's come before. Look at this sentence:

Elizabeth spent many hours planning what she would pack in the van—the van that she had rented for two weeks.

Another time a dash may be used is in defining or giving more information about something in a sentence. Read this sentence:

Margaret knew that when she finally arrived at her sorority house, she would be warmly greeted by her sisters—Bea, Kwila, and Arlene.

The last example could also be punctuated by using parentheses or a colon in place of the dash. You might have written the same sentence this way:

Margaret knew that when she finally arrived at her sorority house, she would be warmly greeted by her sisters (Bea, Kwila, and Arlene).

or this way:

Margaret knew that when she finally arrived at her sorority house, she would be warmly greeted by her sisters: Bea, Kwila, and Arlene.

You can see that punctuating the sentence with a colon is much stuffier than using a dash or parentheses. Generally speaking, save the colon for formal writing.

Dashes with Numbers

Use a special dash, known as an en dash, between two dates and between two page numbers:

Prohibition (1919–1933) came about as a result of the Eighteenth Amendment.

See the section on the Roaring Twenties (pp. 31–35) for more information.

Both of these instances use an en dash, which is longer than a hyphen and shorter than a normal dash, which is usually called an "em dash." Are you confused? Don't be. Most computer programs have an Insert Symbol option that you can use to access en dashes, em dashes, slashes, as well as other symbols.

THE SLASH

A slash is also called a *virgule* and a *solidus*. A virgule/slash/solidus is commonly used to mean *or*. Thus:

a slash/virgule/solidus = a slash or virgule or solidus
You may bring your spouse/significant other to the picnic. = You may bring your spouse or significant other to the picnic.

In mathematics, the slash means *per*, as in this sentence:

There are 5,280 feet/mile.

It's also used in fractions:

$^{365}/_{296}$ *(meaning 365 divided by 296)*

In literature, the slash separates lines of poetry that are written in a block style, as in this passage from Edgar Allan Poe's "The Raven":

"Once upon a midnight dreary, while I pondered, weak and weary, / Over many a quaint and curious volume of forgotten lore— /"

Because of the popularity of the Internet, today the most common use of a slash is in URLs. If you've ever inadvertently omitted a slash when you're typing an address, you know that getting the site to open is impossible.

PARENTHESES

Adding Extra Info

You know what parentheses are, but you may not be completely sure of when and how to use them. You may know very little about square brackets, which, after all, are only used infrequently. Using parentheses tells readers that you're giving some extra information, something that isn't necessary to the meaning of the sentence but is helpful in understanding what's being read. For example:

For a complete study of Hitchcock's movies, see Chapter 8 (pages 85–96).

When readers see parentheses, they know that the material enclosed is extraneous to the meaning of the sentence. If the information is necessary for the sentence to be read correctly, you shouldn't use parentheses. For instance, if you're comparing statistics about two floods that occurred in different years, you might have a sentence like this:

The high-water mark of the 2008 flood came in early April, as compared to the high-water mark of the 1956 flood, which occurred in late May.

You can't put *of the 2008 flood* or *of the 1956 flood* in parentheses because you need that information for the sentence. However, if you have a sentence written like this:

I haven't recovered from my latest (and, I hope, my last) adventure with blind dates.

You could omit the material inside the parentheses and you'd still have the essence of the sentence. Granted, the sentence wouldn't be as cleverly worded, but the gist would be the same.

Another time parentheses are commonly used is in citing dates, especially birth and death dates.

Dame Agatha Christie (1890–1976) wrote twelve novels featuring Miss Marple.

In addition, use parentheses to enclose numbers or letters that name items in a series. Sometimes both the parentheses marks are used, and sometimes just the mark on the right-hand side is used:

Before checking the patient, you should (a) wash your hands; (b) make sure the patient's chart is nearby; (c) call for the attending nurse to supervise.

Before checking the patient, you should a) wash your hands; b) make sure the patient's chart is nearby; c) call for the attending nurse to supervise.

Whether you use both parentheses or just one, be consistent. Also, be aware that if you use one parenthesis only, your reader may easily get the letter mixed up with the preceding word.

In material that covers politics, you'll often see parentheses used to give a legislator's party affiliation and home state (in the case of national politics) or city or county (in the case of state politics).

Senator Willa Liberi (D-RI) met in her Washington office with a number of constituents, including Representative Mark Digery (R-Providence).

Another—though less common—use for parentheses is to show readers that an alternate ending for a word may be read. Take a look at this sentence:

Please bring your child(ren) to the company picnic.

Keep in mind that parentheses would not be used this way in more formal writing; the sentence would be reworded to include both *child* and *children*.

SQUARE BRACKETS

Ordinarily, square brackets aren't used very often, except in dictionaries. A detailed dictionary will often use brackets to show the etymology, or the history, of the word being defined. (Now be honest—you've never noticed brackets in dictionaries, have you?)

One use of square brackets is to make certain that quoted material is clear or understandable for readers. Suppose you're quoting a sentence that contains a pronoun without its antecedent, as in this example:

"He burst onto the party scene and began to take society by storm."

Just who is *he*? Unless the previous sentences had identified him, readers wouldn't know. In that case, you'd use square brackets this way:

"He [Justin Lake] burst onto the party scene and began to take society by storm."

Here's another example:

"It came as a big surprise to everyone at the party."

Readers would have no idea what *it* was. An announcement of retirement? an unexpected large check? a stripper popping out of a cake?

To explain the pronoun so that readers understand the material more clearly, you might use brackets in this way:

"It [the fact that a thief was in their midst] came as a big surprise to everyone at the party."

Along the same lines, you use brackets to alter the capitalization of something you're quoting so that it fits in your sentence or paragraph. For example:

"The river's bank has eroded sufficiently to warrant major repair."

Use brackets for quoted material only if their use doesn't change the meaning of what's being quoted.

Grammar Facts

Remember! Just as with love and marriage and that horse and carriage, you can't have one side of parentheses or brackets without the other (except in display lists).

Another time that brackets are used occurs even less frequently. If you need to give information that you'd normally put in parentheses—but that information is already in parentheses—use brackets instead. This may sound confusing, but take a look at this and you'll see how the rule applies:

The man responsible for the arrest (James Bradson [1885–1940]) was never given credit.

Normally, you put a person's birth and death dates in parentheses, but since those dates are placed in material that's already in parentheses, you use brackets instead.

Depending on the type of writing you do, you might add the Latin word *sic* to the information that you're quoting. You don't know what *sic* means? *Sic* shows that what you're quoting has a mistake that you're copying. By seeing the *sic* designation, readers know that the mistake was made by the original author and not you. Look at this sentence:

"This painting was donated to the museum on September 31 [sic]."

Now, you know and I know that "thirty days hath September"—not thirty-one, as stated in the example. By using [*sic*], readers can tell that you copied the mistake as it was written in the original form. Note that *sic* is enclosed in brackets (many handbooks or style guides dictate that it be italicized as well).

Most style guides allow you to use either brackets or parentheses to let readers know that you've added italics to quoted material. The only rule is that you keep using the same choice of punctuation throughout the manuscript.

Take your pick:

"The time of the accident is as equally important as is the date [italics added]."

"The time of the accident is as equally important as is the date (italics added)."

Generally speaking, you'll use brackets rarely—unless you're writing in a particular style. As with any writing, if you're told to use a particular style guide (say, for instance, *The Chicago Manual of Style*), consult it for the other infrequent times that brackets are used.

ELLIPSIS POINTS

Something Is Missing

Ellipsis points or marks (three spaced periods) let readers know that some material from a quotation has been omitted. Look at this sentence:

Marilyn asked Frank to pick up a hat she had ordered and to stop for milk at the grocery store.

If you needed to quote that sentence but the part about Frank picking up the hat had no relevance to what you were saying, you could use ellipsis points in this way:

Marilyn asked Frank . . . to stop for milk at the grocery store.

You should use ellipsis points only if the meaning of the sentence isn't changed by what you omit.

Suppose you have this sentence:

The policeman reported, "The car involved in the accident had been stolen and then driven by a woman whom friends called 'Honest Harriet.'"

You shouldn't use ellipsis marks to shorten it this way:

The policeman reported, "The car involved in the accident had been . . . driven by a woman whom friends called 'Honest Harriet.'"

In doing so you would've left out some rather vital information.

If the material you're omitting occurs at the end of a sentence, or if you omit the last part of a quoted sentence but what is left remains grammatically complete, use four ellipsis points, with the first one functioning as a period. Take this original passage:

"A number of new people have joined the secret club. In fact, its membership has never been higher. Because the club is devoted to reading classical literature, however, its secret enrollment numbers haven't been questioned by the public at large."

Grammar Facts

Ellipsis marks can also be used in a story to show when a character has lost his train of thought, for example:

His lack of clear direction is disturbing in toda . . . is that a chicken?

You could use ellipsis marks in this way:

"A number of new people have joined the secret club. . . . Because the club is devoted to reading classical literature, however, its secret enrollment numbers haven't been questioned by the public at large."

Another use for ellipsis marks comes if you're quoting someone and trying to show that there's a deliberate pause in what the person said. Read the following paragraph:

Jimmy thought to himself, "If I can just hold on to the ball long enough to get it over to Mike, I know he can get the shot off. . . . I have to pace myself. . . . Twenty-five seconds . . . Fifteen seconds . . . Eight seconds . . . Time for a pass."

The ellipsis marks tell your readers that Jimmy wasn't interrupted by anything, he just didn't have any conscious thoughts in the intervening time indicated by the ellipsis marks.

ITALICS AND UNDERLINING

A Little Added Emphasis

What's the difference between underlining and italics? None. As a reader, you understand the same code when you see italics or underlining. With the use of computers, clicking a button and italicizing a word is just as easy as underlining it. But sometimes (if you're writing longhand or using a typewriter), the option to italicize isn't available. Just remember to consistently use either underlining or italicizing throughout your document. A good idea is to ask if your instructor or company has a policy regarding a preference for italicizing or underlining. (Just so you know, the standard is normally to italicize, rather than to underline.)

So when is italicizing or underlining used? The most common use is in titles, but only titles of long works, such as books. For titles of short works—such as short stories, short poems, and essays—use quotation marks. In the following example, the first bulleted item shows the format for the name of a book; the second bullet shows the name of a short story within that book:

- *The Complete Sherlock Holmes* or <u>The Complete Sherlock Holmes</u>
- "The Adventure of the Speckled Band"

Titles of sacred books don't require any punctuation, nor do books of the Bible.

I read the Bible for a half an hour today.
A copy of the Koran was on his bedside table.

Here's a more complete list of works that should be italicized (underlined):

- Book-length poems and collections of poems: *Leaves of Grass*
- Plays: *A Raisin in the Sun*
- Operas: *Carmen*
- Movies: *Casablanca*
- Pamphlets: *What to Do Before You See the Doctor*
- Television programs (the title of an episode from a program uses quotation marks): *The Walking Dead*
- Works of art: *Mona Lisa*
- Long musical works (a CD would be italicized or underlined; a song from the CD uses quotation marks): *Greatest Love Songs of the New Century*
- Magazines and newspapers (only capitalize and italicize "magazine" if that word is part of the actual title of the periodical; an article title from the magazine or newspaper would have quotation marks around it): *Time*, the *New York Times Magazine*
- Ships, aircraft, spacecraft, trains: *Titanic*, USS *Cole* (don't italicize the USS); *Spirit of St. Louis*; *Endeavor*; *Orient Express*

Keep in mind that articles (*a*, *an*, and *the*) are italicized (underlined) only when they're part of the actual title, except for magazines and newspapers. For instance:

I read Sharyn McCrumb's book The Rosewood Casket.

The is part of the title of the book. On the other hand, you would write:

I spent time aboard the Mir spacecraft.

Mir is the name of the spacecraft; *the* isn't part of its name. However, *the* and *Magazine* are part of the actual name of the following periodical, but *the* is lowercase and not italicized:

I used to do the crossword puzzle in the New York Times
Magazine in pen, but now I do it online.

Emphasis—Another Use of Italics (Underlining)

Look at these sentences and see if you can tell the difference:

"I'm *certain* I'm going to have to arrest you,"
Chief Amanuel Tekle said slyly.
"I'm certain *I'm* going to have to arrest you,"
Chief Amanuel Tekle said slyly.
"I'm certain I'm going to *have* to arrest you,"
Chief Amanuel Tekle said slyly.
"I'm certain I'm going to have to arrest *you*,"
Chief Amanuel Tekle said slyly.
"I'm certain I'm going to have to arrest you,"
Chief Amanuel Tekle said *slyly*.

Can you see that the only difference in the five sentences is the words that are italicized? This illustrates another use of italics. In this case, the use of italics tells readers where emphasis should be placed. This helps the writer let readers know the speech patterns being used, and it also helps readers understand those patterns.

Grammar Facts

Remember that you never use two end marks of punctuation at the end of the sentence.

Be careful not to overuse italics for emphasis. If you use italics or underlining too frequently, you lose the emphasis you want to communicate, and—even worse—your reader soon loses interest. Look at this sentence and you'll see that the device is overdone:

"Chief, the culprit's Mark, not me. I wasn't there when the wreck happened," Bill cried sullenly.

With so many words italicized, the emphasis has lost its effectiveness.

UNUSUAL USAGE

Read the following sentence and see if it makes sense to you:

The angry editor said to the reporter, "You imbecile! You used robbery when you should have used burglary."

Say what? Is the editor telling the reporter that he or she committed the wrong crime? No, and if the writer had used the correct punctuation marks, then the sentence would make sense.

The rule is that when words, numbers, or letters are used outside of their normal context, they should be italicized (underlined). So the sentence really should be written this way:

The angry editor said to the reporter, "You imbecile! You used *robbery* when you should have used *burglary*."

Written this way, readers understand that the reporter used the words *robbery* and *burglary* incorrectly in a story.

Some style guides also mandate that you apply this rule if you're reproducing a sound through a word (if you're using a form of onomatopoeia), as in:

Brrr! I didn't know it was this cold outside
or
When Jerri dropped her new calculator, she cringed as it went *kerplunk* when it landed.

Foreign Terms

The last use of italics is related to the previous one. This rule says you should italicize or underline a foreign word or phrase.

I was wavering about whether to go to the festival with my friends, but I decided *carpe diem*.

If a foreign word or phrase has become so widely used in English that readers wouldn't question its meaning (like per diem or summa cum laude), don't italicize it.

Be careful to apply italics only to punctuation (commas, periods, question marks, exclamation marks, and the like) if that punctuation is part of the title.

May screamed, "There's never been a better mystery than *The Murder of Roger Ackroyd*!"

The title of the book *The Murder of Roger Ackroyd* has no exclamation point, so the exclamation point shouldn't be italicized.

May screamed, "There's never been a better mystery than *The Murder of Roger Ackroyd!*"

The exclamation point and the ending quotation mark aren't italicized, since they aren't part of the title of the book.

Chapter 4

Main Parts of Speech

Most people can remember their elementary English teachers discussing the parts of speech. In order to construct sound and logical sentences you will need to know these parts of speech as they are the building blocks of good grammar and writing. To understand parts of speech you must not only look at the word itself, but how it is used in the sentence, where it is used in the sentence, and what is its meaning. After all, a word can function as more than one part of speech depending on how it is used in the sentence. This may sound confusing, but it becomes almost second nature once you understand the basic parts of speech and what they represent. Of all the words we have in our language there are only eight main parts of speech: nouns, pronouns, verbs, adjectives, adverbs, prepositions, conjunctions, and interjections.

THE NOUN

What a Sentence Is About

A noun simply names a person (*Sammy, man*), place (*Philadelphia, city*), or thing (*Toyota, car*). Some definitions of *noun* also include another category: idea (e.g., *philosophy, warmth*). For purposes of capitalization and points of grammar, nouns are divided into various categories. Knowing the terms will come in handy when you get to the discussion of subject-verb agreement.

Notice that some of the nouns mentioned in the previous paragraph were capitalized and some weren't. Proper nouns (particular persons, places, things, or ideas) are capitalized, but common nouns (everyday names of places, things, or ideas) aren't.

PROPER NOUN	COMMON NOUN
February	month
Egypt	country

Nouns are also classified as concrete or abstract. Concrete nouns, which most nouns are, name things that can be seen, felt, heard, touched, or smelled (*star, water, album, television*). Abstract nouns name concepts, beliefs, or qualities (*freedom, capitalism, courage*).

Some nouns are called compound nouns; these nouns consist of more than one word but count as only one noun. Look at this name:

Henderson County Community and Technical College

It's a compound noun made up of six words, but it's only one noun (it's only one place).

Nouns are also classified as either count or noncount nouns. Count nouns are persons, places, or things that can be (surprise!)

counted (thirteen *colonies*, seventy-six *trombones*). Noncount nouns are persons, places, or things that can't be counted (*unease, happiness*) and are always singular.

Grammar Facts

Sometimes we use a noun like an adjective. When this happens the noun is called an attributive noun. For example, you can sit on a wood bench. In this sentence wood (while it is a noun) is acting as an adjective for the noun bench. Another example is: a silk scarf. Silk is a noun on its own, but here it is being used to describe the scarf.

Collective nouns are names of persons, places, or things that are sometimes counted as one unit (they're considered to be singular) and sometimes counted separately (they're considered to be plural). *Army, herd,* and *family* are all collective nouns.

The following chart will help clarify these terms:

NOUN TYPES

TYPE	DEFINITION	EXAMPLES
COMMON NOUNS	people, places, and things (not specific)	ocean, dog, book, park, boy, woman
PROPER NOUNS	specific people, places, things	Mount Fuji, Pacific Ocean, Yellowstone Park, Joseph
CONCRETE NOUNS	nouns you can perceive with your senses	apple, sun, cat, painting, bird song
ABSTRACT NOUNS	nouns you cannot perceive with your senses	love, happiness, pride, wealth
COMPOUND NOUNS	nouns that are made up of two or more words	snowflake, ponytail, tablecloth, suitcase

NOUN TYPES

TYPE	DEFINITION	EXAMPLES
NONCOUNT NOUNS	nouns that you cannot count	milk, rain, food, music
COUNT NOUNS	nouns that you can count	book, bottle, bowl, child, ticket
COLLECTIVE NOUNS	nouns that refer to things or people as a unit	audience, herd, team, band
SINGULAR NOUNS	nouns that refer to one person, place, thing, or idea	baby, rabbit, car, computer
PLURAL NOUNS	nouns that refer to more than one person, place, thing, or idea	babies, rabbits, cars, computers
POSSESSIVE NOUNS	nouns that show ownership	Dad's car, Cole's dog, teacher's desk

In a sentence, a noun will act either as a subject or some type of complement (predicate nominative, direct or indirect object of a verb, or object of a preposition).

- *The sunset was beautiful.* (The subject of this sentence is *sunset.*)
- *Cathy is a police officer.* (Here *police officer* is a predicate nominative, completing the verb *is.*)
- *Michael recently bought a new car.* (*Car* is the direct object of *bought.*)
- *George gave Lucy his keys.* (*Lucy* is the indirect object of the verb *gave*; *keys* is its direct object.)
- *Jon and Allison went into the restaurant.* (*Restaurant* is the object of the preposition *into.*)

THE PRONOUN

The Stand-In Noun

The textbook definition of a pronoun is "a word that takes the place of a noun." Okay, just what does that mean? Read this paragraph:

When Mrs. Anne Shreiner came into the room, Mrs. Anne Shreiner thought to Mrs. Anne Shreiner's self, "Is the situation just Mrs. Anne Shreiner, or is the temperature really hot in here?" Mrs. Anne Shreiner went to the window and opened the lower part of the window, only to have a number of mosquitoes quickly fly right at Mrs. Anne Shreiner. Mrs. Anne Shreiner said a few choice words, and then Mrs. Anne Shreiner began swatting the pesky mosquitoes, managing to hit a few of the mosquitoes when the mosquitoes came to rest on Mrs. Anne Shreiner's arm.

Isn't that the most boring paragraph you've ever read? That's because no pronouns were used. Now read the same paragraph, but with pronouns inserted in the right places:

When Mrs. Anne Shreiner came into the room, she thought to herself, "Is it just me, or is it really hot in here?" She went to the window and opened the lower part of it, only to have a number of mosquitoes quickly fly right at her. She said a few choice words, and then she began swatting the pesky mosquitoes, managing to hit a few of them when they came to rest on her arm.

What a difference a few pronouns make!

Like nouns, pronouns are divided into various classifications. To determine a pronoun's classification, follow a simple rule that will help you with all of the parts of speech: Look at the way the word is used in a sentence. Personal pronouns, one of the classifications, represent people or things: *I, me, you, he, him, she, her, it, we, us, they, them.*

I came to see you and him today.

Possessive pronouns show ownership (possession): *mine, yours, hers, his, theirs, ours.*

"These parking spaces are yours; ours are next to the door," the teachers explained to the students.

Demonstrative pronouns point out (demonstrate) someone or something: *this, that, these, those.*

This is his umbrella; that is yours.

Relative pronouns relate one part of the sentence to another: *who, whom, which, that, whose.*

The man whom I almost hit last night was taken to the police station. (*Whom* relates to *man.*)

One country that I'd like to visit someday is France. (*That* relates to *country.*)

Reflexive pronouns (or intensive pronouns) reflect to someone or something else in the sentence: *myself, yourself, himself, herself, itself, ourselves, yourselves, themselves.*

I said I'd do it myself! (*Myself* relates back to *I.*)

You must ask yourself what you would do in such a situation. (*Yourself* relates back to *you.*)

One of the most pretentious mistakes writers and speakers make is using a reflexive pronoun when a simple personal pronoun *(I, me, you, he, him, she, her, it, we, us, they, them)* will do. A simple rule to follow is to refrain from using a reflexive pronoun in a sentence if you haven't already specified whom or what you're talking about. Say what? For instance:

Please call Allan Contlesworth and myself at your earliest convenience.

You haven't said who "myself" is. The word *myself* should be replaced with *me* so that the sentence should be written:

Please call Allan Contlesworth and me at your earliest convenience.

Interrogative pronouns ask a question.

Whom can I turn to in times of trouble?
What in the world was that politician talking about?

Grammar Facts

It is a common misconception that a pronoun in a sentence can only refer to the nearest noun. In fact the distance between the pronoun and the antecedent doesn't matter as long a there is only one antecedent that is logical. For example: *Although the invention of the chocolate chip cookie was unintentional and Mrs. Wakefield actually meant for the chocolate pieces to melt in her batter, it is widely acclaimed as a major discovery in the world of food.* Here the pronoun *it* clearly refers to the invention of the cookie even though the pronoun is far away from that noun.

Indefinite pronouns, contrary to their label, sometimes refer to a definite (specific) person, place, or thing that has already been mentioned in the sentence. Indefinite pronouns include *all, another, any, anyone, anything, everybody, everything, few, many, more, most, much, neither, no one, nobody, none, nothing, one, other, others, several, some, someone,* and *something.*

Keep in mind that *all, any, more, most, none,* and *some* sometimes are singular and sometimes are plural.

THE ADJECTIVE
Gives More Information

The textbook definition of an adjective is "a word that modifies a noun or pronoun." Said a different way, an adjective describes, elaborates on, or gives more information about a person, place, or thing.

One way to determine if a word is an adjective is to ask yourself if the word in question gives you information about a noun or pronoun.

During the earthquake, the framed picture came crashing down.

You think the word *framed* is an adjective, and you ask yourself if it gives you more information about a noun. Since *framed* gives you information about *picture*, and *picture* is a thing (a noun), *framed* must be an adjective.

If that method of checking for an adjective doesn't work for you, try this one: Ask yourself if the word answers which one, what kind of, or how many? In the example, you can see that *framed* answers both *which one?* (which picture? the framed one) and *what kind?* (what kind of picture? the framed one), so it must be an adjective.

Common adjectives (ranked by popularity) in English are:

- good
- new
- first
- last
- long
- great
- little
- own
- other
- old
- right
- big
- high
- different
- small
- large
- next
- early
- young
- important
- few
- public
- bad
- same
- able

A special category of adjectives—articles—consists of just three words: *a*, *an*, and *the*. *A* and *an* are called indefinite articles because they don't indicate anything specific (*a house, an honor*); *the* is called a definite article because it names something specific (*the owl, the transit system*).

Another subcategory of adjectives is called determiners. These are adjectives that make specific the sense of a noun; they help determine to which particular units the nouns are referring (e.g., *the country, those apples, seven pencils*).

Grammar Facts

A proper adjective is an adjective formed from a proper noun: American cars, Chinese dumplings, Italian fashion. Usually proper adjectives need to be capitalized as the proper noun would be, but occasionally a proper adjective has become so commonplace that it no longer needs to be capitalized. For example, venetian blind or teddy bear (it once referred to Teddy Roosevelt).

When you're trying to decide if a word is an adjective, examine the way it's used in your sentence. Take a look at these sentences:

I'll go to either game.
I'll go to either the basketball or the football game.

In the first sentence, *either* gives more information about (modifies) the noun *game*, so it's used as an adjective. In the second sentence, *either* is an indefinite pronoun (referring to the word *game*). Look at these sentences:

The tense situation became much more relaxed when the little boy arrived.

What is the tense of that verb?

In the first sentence, *tense* describes *situation* (a thing), so it's an adjective. Looking at it another way, *tense* answers the question *what kind?* about *situation* (a thing), so it's an adjective. In the second sentence, *tense* is simply a thing, so it's a noun.

THE VERB

An Action Word

Verbs are divided into two main categories: action verbs and verbs of being (or linking verbs). Let's start with the easier of the two, action verbs.

ACTION VERBS

Verbs that express action are action verbs (not too difficult to understand, is it?). Action verbs are the more common verbs, and they're easy to spot. Look at these sentences:

Lynn petted the puppy when Mike brought it home to her.
(*Petted* and *brought* both show action.)

The frog sits on top of the lily pad in the lake.
(*Sits* shows action—well, not much action, but you get the picture.)

Action verbs are divided into two categories: transitive and intransitive. The textbook definition of a transitive verb is "a verb that takes an object." What does that mean? If you can answer *whom?* or *what?* to the verb in a sentence, then the verb is transitive.

I carried the injured boy to the waiting ambulance.

Carried whom or what? Since *boy* answers that question, the verb *carried* is transitive in that sentence.

Exhausted, I sank into the sofa.

Sank whom or what? Nothing in the sentence answers that, so the verb *sank* is intransitive in that sentence.

Knowing about transitive and intransitive verbs can help you with some easily confused verbs, such as *lie* and *lay*, and *sit* and *set*. You'll be able to see that *lie* is intransitive (I lie down), *lay* is transitive (I lay the book down), *sit* is intransitive (I'll sit here), and *set* is transitive (Beth set the vase here).

"BEING" VERBS

Granted, the action verb is easy to spot. But what in the world is meant by a definition that says a verb "expresses being"? That usually means the word is a form of the verb *be*. But that's another problem because, except for *been* and *being*, most forms of *be* don't look remotely like *be*.

It would be nonstandard to say, for instance:

I be sitting on the dock of the bay.

You should say:

I am sitting on the dock of the bay.

In that case, *am* is a form of *be*. Looking at the past tense, it would be nonstandard to say:

Yesterday she be sitting on the dock of the bay.

Instead, you should write:

Yesterday she was sitting on the dock of the bay.

So *was* is a form of *be*.

Here are the forms of be: am, is, are, was, were, be, being, been. These forms also include has been, have been, had been, should have been, may be, might have been, will have been, should be, will be, may have been, and might be.

Grammar Facts

Sometimes a verb can have more than one part. A multipart verb has a base or main part and then additional helping (or auxiliary) verbs. For example:

Luke spilled his drink on Katie's desk.
(*spilled* is the main verb)

Because Luke is clumsy, he is always spilling his drinks.
(here *is* and *spilling* work together)

Luke might have spilled his drink on Katie's desk.
(*might have spilled* is a multipart verb group)

UNUSUAL LINKING VERBS
AND HELPING VERBS

Notice that the definition for "be verbs" says they "usually" are forms of "be." Just to complicate the situation, the words in the following list can sometimes be used as linking verbs.

The following verbs can be either linking verbs or action verbs:

- appear
- become
- feel
- grow
- look
- prove
- remain
- seem
- smell
- sound
- stay
- taste

So when are these twelve verbs action verbs, and when are they linking verbs? Use this test: If you can substitute a form of *be* (*am*, *is*, *was*, and so on) and the sentence still makes sense, by golly, you've got yourself a linking verb. Look at these examples:

The soup tasted too spicy for me.

Substitute *was* or *is* for *tasted* and you have this sentence:

The soup was (is) too spicy for me.

It makes perfect sense. You have a linking verb. Now look at this one:

I tasted the spicy soup.

Substitute *was* or *is* for *tasted* and you have this sentence:

I was (is) the spicy soup.

That doesn't make much sense, does it? Since the substitution of a *be* verb doesn't make sense, you don't have a linking verb. You can try the same trick by substituting a form of *seem*:

The soup tasted too spicy for me.

Substitute *seemed* and you have the following:

The soup seemed too spicy for me.

The sentence makes sense, so *tasted* is a linking verb.
If you try the same trick with this sentence:

I tasted the spicy soup.

You get:

I seemed the spicy soup.

That doesn't make sense, so *tasted* isn't a linking verb in this sentence.

Another type of verb that may appear in a sentence is a helping (auxiliary) verb. This can join the main verb (becoming the helper of the main verb) to express the tense, mood, and voice of the verb. Common helping verbs are *be, do, have, can, may,* and so on. (The first two sentences of this paragraph have helping verbs: *may* and *can*.)

THE PRINCIPAL PARTS OF VERBS

You may be familiar with the phrase "the principal parts of verbs," a reference to basic forms that verbs can take. English has four principal parts: the present infinitive (the one that's the main entry in a dictionary), the past tense, the past participle, and the present participle. Take a look at the principal parts of these verbs:

PRESENT INFINITIVE	PAST TENSE	PAST PARTICIPLE	PRESENT PARTICIPLE
hammer	hammered	hammered	hammering
bring	brought	brought	bringing
rise	rose	risen	rising

The first word forms its past and past participle by adding *-ed* to the present infinitive. Most English verbs do this; they're called regular verbs. The last two examples, however, aren't formed in the regular way; these are called (surprise!) irregular verbs. All verbs form the present participle by adding *-ing* to the present infinitive.

THE ADVERB

Elaboration at Its Finest

An adverb is a word that modifies (describes, elaborates on) a verb, adjective, or other adverb. Usually adverbs end in *-ly*, particularly those that are used to express how an action is performed. However, not all adverbs end in *ly*; for example, take: *fast, never, well, very, more, least, now, far, there, quite*, and so on. Adverbs answer one of these questions in a sentence:

- How? (peacefully, happily, angrily)
- When? (tomorrow, yesterday, now)
- Where? (here, there)
- To what degree? (fastest, farthest)
- Why? (usually an adverb clause such as "because she wanted the dog")

For example:

Yesterday the quite relieved soldier very quickly ran out of the woods when he saw his comrade frantically waving at him.

The adverbs in that sentence are *yesterday* (modifies the verb *ran*), *quite* (modifies the adjective *relieved*), *very* (modifies the adverb *quickly*), *quickly* (modifies the verb *ran*), and *frantically* (modifies the verb *waving*).

If you still need help finding adverbs, try this method: Ask yourself if the word you're wondering about answers one of these questions: *how, when, where, why, under what circumstances, how much, how often*, or *to what extent*?

In the example, *yesterday* answers the question *when?*; *quite* answers the question *to what extent?*; *very* answers the question *to what extent?* (or *how much?*); *quickly* answers the question *how?* (or *to what extent?*); and *frantically* answers the question *how?*

Grammar Facts

Want a simple and fun way to remember the purpose and function of adverbs? Check out the classic *Schoolhouse Rock!* song, "Lolly, Lolly, Lolly, Get Your Adverbs Here!" This classic TV episode will make the concept of adverbs easy to remember and the tune will get stuck in your head so you'll never forget it.

Adverbs can also modify adjectives and other adverbs, for example:

She had an extremely white complexion.

Here *extremely* modifies the adjective *white.*

He ran the race remarkably quickly.

Here the adverb *remarkably* modifies the adverb *quickly.*

Following is a list of some of the more common adverbs:

- accidentally
- always
- angrily
- anxiously
- awkwardly
- badly
- blindly
- boastfully
- boldly
- bravely
- brightly
- cheerfully
- coyly
- crazily
- defiantly
- deftly
- deliberately
- devotedly
- doubtfully
- dramatically
- dutifully
- eagerly
- elegantly
- enormously
- evenly
- eventually
- exactly
- faithfully
- finally
- foolishly
- fortunately
- frequently
- gleefully
- gracefully
- happily
- hastily
- honestly
- hopelessly
- hourly
- hungrily
- innocently
- inquisitively
- irritably
- jealously
- justly
- kindly
- lazily
- loosely
- madly
- merrily
- mortally
- mysteriously
- nervously
- never
- obediently
- obnoxiously
- occasionally
- often
- only
- perfectly
- politely
- poorly
- powerfully
- promptly
- quickly
- rapidly
- rarely
- regularly
- rudely
- safely
- seldom
- selfishly
- seriously
- shakily
- sharply
- silently
- slowly
- solemnly
- sometimes
- speedily
- sternly
- technically
- tediously
- unexpectedly
- usually
- victoriously
- vivaciously
- warmly
- wearily
- weekly
- wildly
- yearly

CONJUNCTIVE ADVERBS

Conjunctive adverbs are in a category of their own. These words join independent clauses into one sentence. Here are common conjunctive adverbs:

- accordingly
- furthermore
- instead
- next
- also
- hence
- likewise
- otherwise
- besides
- however
- meanwhile
- still
- consequently
- incidentally
- moreover
- therefore
- finally
- indeed
- nevertheless
- thus

Use conjunctive adverbs to join short sentences into complex thoughts; however, (did you notice the conjunctive adverb there?) be sure that:

1. You have a complete thought on either side of the conjunctive adverb
2. You put a semicolon before it and a comma after it
3. You're joining two closely related thoughts
4. You've used the right conjunctive adverb

English has a small group of adverbs known as intensifiers or qualifiers. These words increase the intensity of the adjectives and other adverbs they modify. Common intensifiers are *awfully, extremely, kind of, more, most, pretty, quite, rather, really, somewhat, sort of, very,* and *too.*

THE PREPOSITION

Describing the Relationship of Nouns

A preposition is a word that links a noun or pronoun to some other word in a sentence. Take, for example, these short sentences:

Jack and Jill went up the hill.
(*Up* is a preposition connecting *went* and *hill.*)
Little Jack Horner sat in a corner.
(*In* is a preposition connecting *sat* and *corner.*)
Sing a song of sixpence.
(*Of* is a preposition connecting *song* and *sixpence.*)

Here are the most common prepositions:

- about
- behind
- down
- off
- to
- above
- below
- during
- on
- toward
- across
- beneath
- except
- onto
- under
- after
- beside
- for
- out
- underneath
- against
- between
- from
- outside
- until
- along
- beyond
- in
- over
- up
- among
- but
- inside
- past
- upon
- around
- by
- into
- since
- with
- at
- concerning
- like
- through
- within
- before
- despite
- of
- throughout
- without

Some prepositions (called compound prepositions) consist of more than one word, like *in spite of, next to, on top of,* and *together with.*

If you're trying to determine if a particular word is a preposition, here's a little trick that works for many prepositions: See if the word will fit in this sentence:

It went _____ the thing(s).

If the word in question makes sense in that sentence, it's a preposition. (Note that *of* is the most notable exception.)

Here's another way of remembering what a preposition is. Look at the last eight letters of the word *preposition*; they spell *position*. A preposition sometimes tells the position of something: *under, over, above,* and so forth.

Here's a rule you've probably heard: Never end a sentence with a preposition. Well, sometimes that rule is correct and sometimes it isn't. Generally, your writing sounds better if you can structure a sentence so that it doesn't end with a preposition. However, sometimes you want a more colloquial or conversational tone, and—let's face it—in speaking, we often end sentences with prepositions.

With whom are you going to the party?

That's the "no-preposition-at-the-end" construction.

Whom are you going to the party with?

That's the way the sentence normally is said.

One important thing to remember about prepositions is that they are always in prepositional phrases. A prepositional phrase consists of a noun (or pronoun) and a preposition. The noun is the object of the preposition.

The coat is inside the closet.

Closet is the object of the preposition *inside*.

A prepositional phrase can also contain adjectives and adverbs but the main ingredients are the preposition and the noun.

Grammar Facts

If a preposition is not used in an prepositional phrase then it is not a preposition! A preposition must always be in a phrase; if not, then you have some other part of speech. For example:

The car went down the hill. (*down* is a preposition here with the noun *hill*.)

Put the baby down! (*down* is not a preposition in this sentence because it is not in a phrase. It is an adverb.)

THE CONJUNCTION

Hooking Up Words

A conjunction joins words in a sentence; that is, it provides a junction between words. Conjunctions are divided into three categories: coordinating, correlative, and subordinating.

Coordinating conjunctions are the conjunctions that most people think of when they think of conjunctions. These words join words, phrases, and independent clauses.

These conjunctions are easy to remember if you remember the mnemonic device FANBOYS:

- For
- And
- Nor
- But
- Or
- Yet
- So

Sometimes these coordinating conjunctions will be preceded by a comma and sometimes not. Here is an easy rule to remember about comma usage: If the conjunction is joining two independent phrases (meaning they could stand on their own), then you should use a comma.

Grammar Facts

Some traditional grammarians believe it is incorrect to start a sentence with a coordinating conjunction. While that may be true some of the time, in today's world it has certainly become more acceptable to do so, especially if it helps break up a long sentence.

Correlative conjunctions can't stand alone; they must have a "relative" nearby in the same sentence. You might think of these as "tag-team" conjunctions; you have to have both of them in different parts of the sentence for the sentence to work. They get their name from the fact that they have to work together (co-) to relate meaning. Correlative conjunctions include:

- both/and
- either/or
- neither/nor
- not only/also
- not only/but also

- such/that
- as/as
- rather/than
- as many/as
- no sooner/than

I will *either* take my car to the mechanic *or* try and fix it myself.
Neither the pollen outside *nor* the dust inside is making me sneeze.
I would *no sooner* take that job *than* eat dog food.

Subordinating conjunctions are often the most difficult conjunctions to recognize. They are used in the beginning of dependent clauses (words that have a subject and verb but which cannot stand alone as sentences) to join that clause to the main clause. You may remember that dependent clauses are sometimes called subordinate clauses. The meaning of the subordinate clause is dependent on the main clause; it has no meaning on its own.

The most common ones are the following:

- after
- how
- than
- although
- if
- that
- as in
- in order that
- though
- as if
- in that

- unless
- as long as
- inasmuch as
- until
- as much as
- now that
- when
- as soon as
- once
- where
- assuming that

- providing that
- whenever
- because
- since
- wherever
- before
- so long as
- whether
- even though
- so that
- while

Here are some subordinating conjunctions at work:

You can get up from the table *once* you've finished your vegetables.
Because her hands were freezing, Karen put on her gloves.
I sneeze loudly *whenever* I see the sun.

THE INTERJECTION

Standalone Emotions

Egads! You don't remember what an interjection is? It's a word or phrase that expresses surprise or some other emotion or is used as filler. An interjection often stands alone (*gosh, darn*). If an interjection is part of a sentence, it doesn't have a relation to other words in the sentence; if it's taken out of the sentence, the meaning is unchanged. Take a look at these sentences:

Hey, dude.
Like, what's going on?
Ouch! Did you step on my toe?

Hey, *like*, and *ouch* are interjections.

When you're expressing a strong emotion or surprise (as in *Stop!* or *Darn it all!*), use an exclamation point. If you're using milder emotion or merely using a filler (as in *like* or *well*), use a comma.

Grammar Facts

Interjections that are considered too off-color for readers are often denoted by using various symbols, in no particular order. For example, *"I've been stood up by that $@*# guy for the last time!" Lolita cried.*

A note of caution about interjections: use them in moderation, if at all. In dialogue, interjections are used far more often than in more formal writing, where they're hardly ever used.

Here are common interjections in the English language:

- ah
- aha
- ahem
- ahoy
- alack
- alas
- all hail
- alleluia
- aloha
- amen
- attaboy
- aw
- ay
- bah
- behold
- bejesus
- bingo
- bleep
- boo
- bravo
- bye
- cheerio
- cheers
- ciao
- crikey
- cripes
- dear
- doh

- duh
- eh
- encore
- eureka
- fie
- gee
- gee whiz
- gesundheit
- goodness
- gosh
- great
- hah
- ha-ha
- hail
- hallelujah
- heigh-ho
- hello
- hem
- hey
- hi
- hip
- hmm
- ho
- ho hum
- hot dog
- howdy
- huh
- humph

- hurray
- hush
- indeed
- jeepers
  creepers
- jeez
- lo and
  behold
- man
- my word
- now
- ooh
- oops
- ouch
- phew
- phooey
- pshaw
- rats
- righto
- scat
- shoo
- shoot
- so
- so long
- there
- touché
- tush
- tut

- tut-tut
- ugh
- uh-huh
- uh-oh
- uh-uh
- viva
- voilà
- wahoo
- well
- what
- whoa
- whoopee
- whoops
- whoosh
- wow
- yay
- yes
- yikes
- yippee
- yo
- yoicks
- yoo-hoo
- yuk
- yummy
- zap

Chapter 5

Pronouns

Of all the main parts of speech, pronouns often give people the most trouble. Oddly, these words are the smallest words, but they cause a great deal of confusion. Which pronoun do you need to use, which word does it have to agree with, which person should it be? Ironically, some of the biggest snafus in writing and speaking come from misusing these little words. Using the wrong pronouns leaves your reader in doubt as to who or what you are referring to and makes your writing illogical. As handy as they are, pronouns sure can pose some problems for both speakers and writers. Yet using the proper pronoun is necessary to avoid both confusion and miscommunication.

PRONOUN PROBLEMS

Clarity Is Key

Pronouns take the place of nouns and as a result they can do all the things nouns can do; they can be subjects, direct objects, indirect objects, objects of prepositions, and more. The problems with pronouns often come when the writer is not clear about whom the pronoun is referring to. Consider the following:

> *Last night, the suspect was charged with hitting a fellow diner and knocking them to the floor. I spoke to E. J. and Pat earlier today, and I asked her if she had been there when it happened. She said that after the incident, the conversation between the other diners and she centered around thinking about whom would be questioned by the police. All the people who were discussing this they finally decided that if you were there, you probably were going to be questioned.*

Can you point out what's wrong in this paragraph? The story has examples of several common pronoun problems:

- A plural pronoun that refers to a singular antecedent
- A pronoun that isn't clear about which antecedent it refers to
- Pronouns that shift points of view in the same sentence
- A pronoun that's not needed
- A pronoun that's in the wrong case
- Confusion about when to use *who* and *whom*

Maybe it's time to take a look at these pesky pronoun problems. Pronouns, as you know, are words that take the place of nouns. Common pronouns include:

- I
- herself
- both
- me
- itself
- each
- you
- ourselves
- either
- he
- yourselves
- everybody
- him
- themselves
- everyone
- she
- this
- everything
- her
- that
- few
- it
- these
- little
- us
- those
- many
- they
- who
- most
- them
- whom
- much
- mine
- which
- neither
- yours
- whose
- no one
- hers
- what
- nobody
- his
- all
- none
- theirs
- another
- nothing
- ours
- any
- one
- myself
- anybody
- other
- yourself
- anyone
- others
- himself
- anything
- several
- some
- somebody
- someone

PROBLEMS WITH AGREEMENT: A NUMBERS GAME

Pronouns must agree in number with the words to which they refer (their antecedents). Read these sentences:

After I read the letters, I tossed it in the wastebasket.
After I read the letters, I tossed them in the wastebasket.

The first sentence doesn't make sense because *it* is the wrong pronoun. The noun that *it* refers to is *letters*, and *letters* is a plural noun. The pronoun used to replace *it* should also be plural. In the second sentence, *it* has been replaced by *them*, which is plural. That's why the second sentence makes sense.

Put another way, the rule is this: If a pronoun is plural, the word it refers to (also known as its antecedent) must be plural; if a pronoun is singular, the word it refers to must be singular.

So what's the problem? Complications arise where some of the indefinite pronouns are concerned.

PROBLEMS WITH INDEFINITE PRONOUNS

Indefinite pronouns include the following:

- all
- everyone
- none
- another
- everything
- nothing
- any
- few
- one
- anybody
- little
- other
- anyone
- many
- others
- anything
- most
- several
- both
- much
- some
- each
- neither
- somebody
- either
- no one
- someone
- everybody
- nobody
- something

Anyone, anybody, anything, each, either, everybody, everyone, everything, neither, nobody, none, no one, one, somebody, something, and *someone* are all considered to be singular words, so they all require a singular pronoun. But, if you think about it, the word *each* implies more than one. If each person is doing something, that means more than one, right? The same can be said for *everybody, everything*, and *everyone*. This doesn't matter; all four words are considered singular. So you should write:

> *Everybody is seated, and each is waiting for the plane to take off.*
> *Each of the dogs needs its collar before it can be enrolled in*
> *obedience school.*

> *Everyone must bring a list of her prenatal vitamins. (Using only*
> her *in this sentence is perfectly fine since no men would be taking*
> *prenatal vitamins.)*

A common tendency in everyday speech is to use *they* or *their* in place of some singular pronouns. In the first example, you might hear the sentence spoken this way:

> *Everybody is seated, and they are waiting for the plane to take off.*

This usage is called the "singular they" because *they* refers to an antecedent that's singular.

Even though using the "singular they" is becoming more commonplace, its usage is still frowned on in many circles. However, this may be one of the rules of grammar that eventually changes. The advocates of the "singular they" point out that using it helps prevent an overuse of *his or her* or *he or she*.

Now it's time to break a rule. Remember the one that says to disregard any prepositional phrase when you're looking for the subject of a sentence? Well, this rule has a few exceptions. (This is also discussed in Chapter 8 about subject-verb agreement.) Take a look at these two sentences:

> *All of the money is missing from the safe.*
> *All of the cookies are missing from the jar.*

In both sentences, the subject is *all*. But the first sentence has a singular verb and the second sentence has a plural verb—and both are correct.

With five pronouns (*all, any, most, none,* and *some*), the "disregard the prepositional phrase" rule is canceled out. For those five pronouns, look at the object of the preposition to determine which verb to use.

Grammar Facts

When you have compound antecedents that are joined by *or* or *nor* (or *either . . . or, neither . . . nor*), make the pronoun agree with the one that's closer to the verb. Here's an example:

Either the lion or the monkeys have already gotten their food.

Since *monkeys* is plural and it comes nearer the pronoun, use the plural pronoun *their*.

Either the monkeys or the lion has already gotten its food.

Since *lion* is singular and it comes nearer the pronoun, use the singular pronoun *its*.

So, do you think you can pinpoint the mistake in the following paragraph? Pronouns and their antecedents should agree in number.

When I came down to breakfast, everybody in the family was eating, but nobody offered me even a piece of toast. At work, everyone was busy doing their different projects; they didn't even stop to look up when I came in.

By changing the incorrect pronouns, you should have:

When I came down to breakfast, everybody in the family was eating, but nobody offered me even a piece of toast. At work, everyone was busy doing his or her different projects; they didn't even stop to look up when I came in.

You can see, though, that there's a definite problem with that rewriting. While it may be grammatically correct, it sure doesn't read well. Contrary to rules of thirty or more years ago, using *his or her* rather than just *his* is now considered correct. But as you can see in the corrected paragraph, this can make for some rather awkward writing.

So what can you do to prevent this awkwardness? Rewriting the sentences to use plural nouns and pronouns instead of singular ones is far better. The paragraph could be rewritten this way:

When I came down to breakfast, all of my family were already eating, but nobody offered me even a piece of toast. At work, all of my associates were already busy doing their different projects; they didn't even stop to look up when I came in.

Much better, isn't it?

VAGUE PRONOUN REFERENCES

Whom Are We Talking About?

One of the most common writing problems occurs in sentences that have unclear antecedents of the pronouns.

As you recall, pronouns are words that take the place of nouns; antecedents are the nouns that the pronouns refer to. For example:

Chelsea called to say she and Anthony would be glad to help decorate.

In this sentence, the pronoun *she* refers to *Chelsea*; therefore, *Chelsea* is the antecedent of *she*. Now, look at this example:

The movie's humor was rather sophomoric, and it didn't go over well with most of the audience.

The pronoun *it* refers to *humor*; *humor* is the antecedent of *it*.

In these examples, the antecedents are used correctly. They clearly refer to specific nouns (their antecedents). But take a look at this sentence:

Eddie invited Bud to the ranch because he enjoyed horseback riding.

Well, now. Just whom does the word *he* in the second part of the sentence refer to—Eddie or Bud? The antecedent of *he* isn't clear.

To make the sentence read clearly, it should be reworded:

Because Bud enjoyed horseback riding, Eddie invited him to the ranch.
or

Eddie, who enjoyed horseback riding, invited Bud to the ranch.

Now look at these sentences:

Patty called Linda to report the unexpected news that she had gotten a raise. When Patty told Claudia and Lorraine the news, she said that they should celebrate.

Are you confused? Who got the raise—Patty or Linda? Who said that a celebration was in order—Patty or Claudia or Lorraine? Who was to be included in the celebration—Patty, Linda, Claudia, and Lorraine? Linda and Claudia and Lorraine? Patty and Claudia and Lorraine? The way the two sentences are now worded, readers aren't sure.

Grammar Facts

A *vague* pronoun reference is when no specific noun comes before the pronoun. An *ambiguous* pronoun reference happens when more than one noun comes before the pronoun making it difficult to determine which noun the pronoun refers to.

You can correct the first sentence in several ways, depending on whom you're referring to by the words *she* and *they*. Suppose Patty is the one who has received the raise. One way to recast the sentence to express that meaning is this way:

Patty, who had received the unexpected news that she had gotten a raise, called her friend Linda.

Now there's no doubt about who received the raise. If Linda had received the raise, then the sentence could be reworded this way:

Patty called Linda to report the unexpected news that Linda had gotten a raise.

In the second sentence, who's going to celebrate? To make the meaning clearer, that sentence could be reworded this way:

Patty told Claudia and Lorraine the news, and she also said that they all should celebrate.

Now it's clear who announced the celebration and who was to be included in it.

Sometimes a pronoun has no reference at all. Read this sentence:

Cathy Blue was afraid he wouldn't remember to pick up the refreshments for the party.

Just who is *he*? Unless the man has been identified in an earlier sentence, readers are left out in the cold about his identity.

Remember that an antecedent has to refer to a specific person, place, or thing. Look at this sentence:

The young recording star was elated, but he kept it hidden.

What did the star keep hidden? Was *it* supposed to refer to the fact that he felt elated? In that case, the sentence would read:

The young recording star was elated, but he kept elated hidden.

Doesn't make sense, does it? The word *elated* can't be the antecedent of *it* because *elated* isn't a person, place, or thing. The sentence needs to be reworded something like this:

The young recording star was elated with his hit record, but he kept his elation hidden.

Along the same lines, sometimes a sentence has a noun that the pronoun refers to, but it's not the right noun; the correct reference is missing from the sentence. Read this sentence:

After a successful fishing trip with his brothers, Joe let them all go.

The way the sentence is worded, Joe let his brothers go. That's what *them* refers to in this sentence. But surely that's not what happened! What the writer means is that Joe let all the fish go. The sentence should be rewritten like this:

After a successful fishing trip with his brothers, Joe let all of their catch go.

When you're referring to people, use *who*, *whom*, or *whose*, not *which* or *that*. Here's an incorrect sentence:

I'm indebted to the people which helped me during the flood.

Here's the sentence in the correct way:

I'm indebted to the people who helped me during the flood.

Here's another example:

The new tax forms arrived today. They want me to fill out every line on the last three pages.

The tax forms want you to do the filling out? That's silly! What the writer meant was that the Internal Revenue Service, or an accounting firm—someone the writer failed to name—wants the tax forms filled out. The sentence needs to be reworded to make it clear who *they* are.

The new tax forms arrived today. Our accountant wants me to fill out every line on the last three pages.

Be careful not to use *they* when you refer to unnamed persons; *they* must refer to people you specify. The same holds true for any pronoun, but *they*, *he*, *she*, and *it* are the ones most commonly misused. If you think you may have an unclear reference, one way to test the sentence is to do this:

1. Find the pronoun.
2. Replace the pronoun with its antecedent—the noun it refers to.
3. If the sentence doesn't make sense, reword it.

FIRST-, SECOND-, AND THIRD-PERSON PRONOUNS

Consistency Is Key

Both pronouns and points of view are expressed in first person, second person, and third person. First-person pronouns include *I, me, my, mine, we, our, ours,* and *us,* and the first-person point of view expresses the personal point of view of the speaker or author *(I will bring the book).* Second-person pronouns include *you, your,* and *yours,* and material expressed in the second-person point of view directly addresses the listener or reader *(You will bring the book).* Third-person pronouns include *he, she, him, her, his, hers, they, them, their,* and *theirs.* In the third-person point of view material is expressed from the point of view of a detached writer or other characters *(They will bring the book).* If you're in doubt about which point of view to use, use third person.

SHIFTS IN PERSON

One of the most common problems in writing comes with a shift in person. The writer begins in either first or third person and then—without reason—shifts to second person. Take, for example, this paragraph:

> *Even in a casual atmosphere, I can be embarrassed by someone else, and this causes you to become tense. For instance, somebody you know can embarrass you at a party or in a class. It's so simple for a stranger to embarrass you.*

What's wrong with that paragraph? The writer begins in the first person (telling about himself or herself by using the pronoun *I*) and then shifts to second person. The constant use of *you* sounds as if the writer is preaching directly to readers. That writer doesn't know the readers and doesn't know if he or she can be easily embarrassed by others, and so on. Except for the beginning sentence, the entire paragraph should be rewritten and put into first person. Here is one way of doing that:

> *Even in a casual atmosphere, I can be embarrassed by someone else, and this causes me to become tense. For instance, somebody I know can embarrass me at a party or in a class. It's so simple for a stranger to embarrass me.*

Repeat three times: Consistency is the key. Consistency is the key. Consistency is the key. If you begin in third person (which is the most common way of writing), stay in third person. If you begin in first person (the second most common way of writing), stay in first person. If you begin in second person, stay in second person. Consistency is the key.

Grammar Facts

Writers often can't decide whether to use *we* or *us* when the pronoun comes right before a noun, as in these examples:

> "(We, Us) seniors decided to play a prank on you," Matt told his instructors.

> "You'd better rethink any decision to play a prank on (we, us) teachers," came the sharp reply.

To determine which pronoun is correct, just delete the noun that the pronoun refers to (*seniors* in the first sentence, *teachers* in the second sentence) and see how you would say the sentence.

(You did notice that the preceding paragraph is written in second person, didn't you? Actually, the first sentences are in second person. They're written in what's called a "you understood" form: Even though the word *you* isn't included in the sentences, it's implied and readers understand that *you* is the subject of each sentence.)

USING THE SECOND PERSON

For various reasons, most instructors usually disapprove of second person in formal writing. Is using second person ever acceptable? It is when you need an informal tone. Read something written in second person (remember, that means using *you* and *your*), and you'll find a more conversational tone than if it had been written in first or third person. Use second person when you want your words to come across in a casual way. Take a look at this paragraph:

You'll need to watch the mixture carefully, and you may have to stir it quite often. When you get to the last step, make sure you add the final three ingredients slowly. If you add them too quickly, you'll have a mess on your hands.

You can easily read that paragraph. It's talking directly to you, telling you what to do in your cooking. But look at the same paragraph written in third person:

The mixture must be watched carefully, and it may have to be stirred quite often. At the last step, it's important that the final three ingredients be added slowly. If they're added too quickly, the combination may create a mess.

Now, that's pretty boring and stilted, isn't it? The directions are far better if you write them in the second person.

Another time that second-person writing is used with frequency is in advertising. Consider this sign:

Come see the friendly folks at Abbotts' Used Car Lot!

That's more inviting than if it were written in the third person:

Readers of this sign are invited to come see the friendly folks at Abbotts' Used Car Lot!

The friendly folks at Abbotts' probably wouldn't have much business with a sign like that, would they?

SUBJECTIVE, OBJECTIVE, AND POSSESSIVE PRONOUNS

Make Your Case

Pronouns are also one of three cases: subjective, objective, and possessive. The way you use a pronoun in a sentence determines which case you should use.

1. **Subjective pronouns** include *I, you, he, she, it, we,* and *they.*
2. **Objective pronouns** include *me, you, him, her, it, us,* and *them.* (Note that *you* and *it* are included on both lists; you'll see why later.)
3. **Possessive pronouns** include *my, your, his, her, its, our,* and *their.* (Possessive pronouns are regarded as adjectives by some grammarians. These pronouns won't be discussed in this section because people rarely have a problem with using them correctly.)

Grammar Facts

What do you do when you want to use a possessive noun and pronoun? You should add an -'s to the noun that comes before the pronoun. For example:

This document has Bill's and my comments.
Tomorrow will be Hillary's, Jackie's, and my last day.
The dog is Scott's and mine.

SUBJECTIVE PRONOUNS

Here's the first part of a no-brainer: Subjective pronouns are used as the subjects of sentences (whom or what you're talking about). You would say, for instance:

I am going to leave for my appointment.
She is late already.

No problem seeing the right form in those sentences, is there? For some reason, though, a problem occasionally arises when subjects are compound. You might read, for instance:

His brothers and him are going to the ball game.

Margaret, Elizabeth, and me were at the mall for four hours yesterday.

Me and her see eye to eye on lots of things.

These pronouns are used incorrectly. Because the pronouns are used as subjects of the sentence, they should all be in the subjective case: *I, you, he, she, it, we,* or *they.* So, the sentences should read:

His brothers and he are going to the ball game.

Margaret, Elizabeth, and I were at the mall for four hours yesterday.

I and she see eye to eye on lots of things. (Actually, etiquette says to put the other person first, so it's better to word this sentence like this: She and I see eye to eye on lots of things.)

If you're not sure if you've used the right pronoun, try writing or saying the sentence with only one subject. You'd never say:

Him is going to the ball game.
Me was at the mall for four hours yesterday.
Me sees eye to eye on lots of things.
Her sees eye to eye on lots of things.

Since those pronouns sound wrong when they're by themselves, you know that they're the wrong case. Change the pronouns to the ones you'd normally use when there's just one subject.

OBJECTIVE PRONOUNS

Objective pronouns are used as the objects in sentences. You would say, for instance:

Hallie and Travis went to see her last night.

When Liz and Marvin celebrated their anniversary, Betty gave them a new CD.

"Give me the money right now!" the robber demanded.

As with compound subjects, problems arise with compound objects. People will write or say sentences like this:

The argument arose last night between Carla and she.

Please buy a raffle ticket from Fr. Hammerstein, Jane Ann, or I.

"The car sped by he and I, going 90 miles per hour," the witness testified.

Again, each pronoun is used incorrectly in these sentences. Because the pronouns are used as objects in these sentences, they should all be in the objective case: *me, you, him, her, it, us,* and *them.* So, the sentences should read:

The argument arose last night between Carla and her.

Please buy a raffle ticket from Fr. Hammerstein, Jane Ann, or me.

"The car sped by him and me, going 90 miles per hour," the witness testified.

Grammar Facts

Remember that pronouns that are predicate nominatives should be subject pronouns. Predicate nominatives, you recall, are nouns or pronouns used after linking verbs (usually forms of *be*, like *am*, *is*, *are*, *was*, and *were*).

The way to test yourself if you're not sure if you've used the right pronoun is to use the same trick that you used for the subjective pronoun problem, but substitute the objective form; that is, write or say the sentence with only one object. You'd never say:

The argument arose last night between she.
Please buy a raffle ticket from I.
"The car sped by he, going 90 miles per hour," the witness testified.
"The car sped by I, going 90 miles per hour," the witness testified.

Since those pronouns sound wrong when they're by themselves, you know that they're the wrong case. Change the pronouns to the ones you'd normally say when the sentence has only one object.

So why were *you* and *it* on the lists of both subjective and objective pronouns? Because, unlike other pronouns on the lists (*I* and *me*, for example), English uses the same form for those two words.

It was nice to get a surprise in the mail. (*It* is a subject.)
I got it in the mail. (*It* is an object.)
You called me at four o'clock? (*You* is a subject.)
I called you back at five o'clock. (*You* is an object.)

SITUATIONS WITH THAN AND AS

Another problem with pronouns sometimes arises in a sentence with words that are omitted following *than* or *as*.

Look at the following examples:

Jim said to Donna, "I always thought Billy liked you more than me."
Jim said to Donna, "I always thought Billy liked you more than I."

When the words that have been omitted after *than* are restored, the real meaning of the sentences becomes clear:

Jim said to Donna, "I always thought Billy liked you more than (he liked) me."
Jim said to Donna, "I always thought Billy liked you more than I (liked you)."

(Either way, Jim's in quite a snit, isn't he?)

The same type of confusion can result when words following *as* have been omitted. For example, someone might say or write something along the lines of:

My husband finds physics as interesting as me.

This implies that, to the husband, physics and his wife are of equal interest. Now, look at the correction:

My husband finds physics as interesting as I (do).

This signifies that both spouses are equally interested in physics—which, one hopes, is the intended meaning here.

By mentally adding the missing verb at the end of a sentence using *than* or *as* in this way, you'll be able to tell which pronoun to use.

WHO AND WHOM

The Perpetual Problem

For many people, deciding whether to use *who* or *whom* may be the most difficult of all the problems with pronouns. Do you say, "The man who I called has already placed an order" or "The man whom I called has already placed an order"? How can you make your mind up between "The student who is early will get the best seat" and "The student whom is early will get the best seat"?

If you have trouble deciding whether to use *who* or *whom* (or *whoever* or *whomever*), try the following method. It substitutes *he* and *him* for *who* and *whom* and provides a mnemonic for remembering when you should use which pronoun.

Grammar Facts

The use of *whom* is gradually decreasing in casual speaking, although many people are still careful about its use. Generally, its use—its correct use—is still important in writing.

First, remember to look only at the clause (a set of words with a subject and its verb) associated with *who* or *whom*. Some sentences have only one clause, and that makes finding the right word easy. Often, though, a sentence has more than one clause (an independent clause and one or more dependent clauses).

Next, scramble the words of the clause (if you have to) so that the words form a statement, not a question.

Now, substitute either *he* or *him* for *who* or *whom*. This will tell you whether to use *who* or *whom*. Use the mnemonic *he* = *who*, *hiM* = *whoM* (the final *m* helps you remember the association). If your sentence is about females only, pretend they're males for the sake of your mnemonic.

Be on the lookout for predicate nominatives. After you scramble the words, if you have a linking verb rather than an action verb, use *he* (*who*) instead of *him* (*whom*).

Ready to put all this to a test? Try this sentence:

(Who, Whom) telephoned late last night?

Since the sentence has only one clause, all you need to do is see if it's necessary to scramble the words to make a statement. In this sentence, no scrambling is necessary. You can substitute *he* and have a perfectly good sentence: *He telephoned late last night.* Since you substituted *he* instead of *him* (remember that *he = who*), you know to use *who* in the original question.

Now, try this example:

(Who, Whom) were you telephoning late at night?

This sentence also has only one clause that you have to deal with. Scramble the words to make a statement; then substitute *he* or *him*, and you have the statement "You were telephoning him late at night." Since you used *him* in the new sentence, you know to use *whom* in the original question.

Grammar Facts

An independent clause is a set of words with a subject and its verb that expresses a complete thought; it could stand alone as a sentence. A dependent clause—while having a subject and verb—makes no sense by itself; it can't stand alone as a sentence.

Now for a trickier example:

Eugene worried about (who, whom) Ike would be teamed with in the competition.

As you can tell, this sentence has two clauses (you could tell that, couldn't you?). Remember that you're *only* concerned with the clause that contains the *who/whom* question. In this case, take the words after *about*, scramble them to make a statement, substitute *he* or *him*, and you have "Ike would be teamed with him in the competition." Since you used *him*, you would know that the original sentence would use *whom* (remember the mnemonic *him* = *whom*). So the original sentence would read this way:

Eugene worried about whom Ike would be teamed with in the competition.

Here's another example that you have to stop and think about:

Was that (who, whom) you thought it was?

When you look *only* at the clause the *who/whom* is concerned with and you substitute *he/him*, you have "it was he/him." A light bulb goes off in your head because you recognize that *was* is a linking verb. That tells you to use *he* (the predicate nominative).

Chapter 6

Additional Parts of Speech

In addition to the eight main parts of speech, English has three other parts (participles, gerunds, and infinitives), which are called verbals. Verbals are called hybrids because they're part verb. However, they don't act as verbs; instead, they act as other parts of speech. This isn't as complicated as it sounds; you probably use verbals all the time without realizing it. Also important are the three main parts of a sentence: a subject, a predicate (verb), and complements (words that complete the meaning of the subject and predicate). Jump right in and see if you can tackle these not-so-tricky trios.

PARTICIPLES

Formed from Verbs but Act Like Adjectives

A participle is part verb and part something else, but it's used as an adjective. In a previous chapter, you learned that adjectives answer one of three questions: *which one? what kind of?* or *how many?* That will come in handy here, too. Participles come in two forms: the present participle and the past participle.

The present participle will always consist of a verb plus *-ing*, as in these sentences:

Let sleeping dogs lie.

Sleeping consists of the verb *sleep* plus the ending *-ing*, and it acts as an adjective in the sentence. It describes *dogs*, and it answers the question *which ones?*

Shivering when they came in, Peter and Sylvia Niblo made a mad dash for the coffeepot.

Shivering consists of the verb *shiver* plus the ending *-ing*, and it acts as an adjective in the sentence. It describes *Peter and Sylvia Niblo*, and it answers the question *what kind of?* or *which one?* The previous examples illustrate present participles.

Past participles of regular verbs consist of a verb plus *-d* or *-ed*, as in these sentences:

Exhilarated from the victory, the entire team embraced the cheering fans.

Exhilarated consists of the verb *exhilarate* plus the ending -*d*, and it acts as an adjective in the sentence. It describes *team*, and it answers the question *which ones?*

> *Stained with both mustard and ketchup, my new shirt went right into the washing machine.*

Stained consists of the verb *stain* plus the ending -*ed*, and it acts as an adjective in the sentence. It describes *shirt*, and it answers the question *which one?* The previous examples illustrate past participles.

So what's the big deal about a participle? Sometimes it's used in the wrong way, and that creates a dangling participle (hanging participle or unattached participle). Take a look at this sentence:

> *Babbling incoherently, the nurse quickly wrapped his arms around the child.*

The way the sentence is written, the nurse was babbling (a participle) incoherently. What the writer means (at least, what we hope he or she means) is that the *child* was babbling incoherently. The sentence should be rewritten, perhaps this way:

> *The nurse quickly wrapped his arms around the babbling child.*

Here's another dangling participle:

> *Tired from shopping at the mall, the recliner looked like the perfect spot for Kathy Wethington.*

How in the world could a recliner have a tiring day shopping? That participle (*tired*) and the rest of the words that go with it (its phrase: *tired from shopping*) should be moved. A better way to word that sentence would be:

The recliner looked like the perfect spot for Kathy Wethington, who was tired from the long day shopping at the mall.

Grammar Facts

The past participles of irregular verbs vary greatly. For example the past participle of *sing* is *sung* and the past participle of *bring* is *brought*. Check your dictionary for any irregular verb past participle.

Participles have three main functions: they can act as adjectives, as direct objects, or as part of a multipart verb.

Past and present participles can act as adjectives, for example:

The mother tried to help the crying baby.

Which baby? The crying baby.

The broken fender, smashed headlight, and bleeding forehead all indicated that Joe had been in an accident.

Which fender? The broken one. Which headlight? The smashed one. Which forehead? The bleeding one.

Participles can also act as direct objects.

Nicholas hates cooking because he has had too many culinary failures.

Cooking is the object of *hates*.

Paul's favorite thing to do in the summer is swimming.

Swimming is the object of the verb *is*.
And finally participles can act as part of a multipart verb as in:

Samantha was running away form the angry dog.

Was is the main verb and *running* is the present participle.

GERUNDS

A Verb That Ends in -ing

A gerund is a word that begins with a verb and ends in -ing. Wait a minute! Isn't that what a present participle is? Glad you were paying attention. Now for the rest of the story. A gerund begins with a verb, ends in -ing, and acts like a noun (that is, it names a person, place, or thing).

Running up hills for the last six months has improved Cathy's stamina.

Running is a gerund. It's composed of a verb (*run*), ends in -ing, and is used as a noun.

Gerunds can appear by themselves or they can be part of a larger gerund phrase, but either way they function as nouns.

Blowing bubbles on a windy day can be disastrous.

Blowing bubbles on a windy day is the gerund phrase subject of the verb *can be*.

Greg hates running on a treadmill.

Running on a treadmill is a gerund phrase that is the direct object of *hates*.

You should always put the possessive noun or possessive pronoun (*my, your, his, her, its, our,* and *their*) before a gerund. For some reason this rule is often ignored or misunderstood by many people, but it is proper grammar. Look at this sentence:

David continues to be amazed by (Susan, Susan's) singing.

Use the possessive *Susan's* before the gerund *singing*.
The same is true for this sentence:

Steve and Diana weren't happy about (us, our) leaving so early.

Use the possessive pronoun *our* before the gerund *leaving*.

Grammar Facts

Look at the different uses of *addressing* in these sentences:

Addressing the problem made Pat Davis realize what she must do.

Addressing the audience, Donna and Jim White felt a connection.

Anthony and Ruth Hazelwood mailed the invitations as soon as they finished addressing the envelopes.

In the first sentence, *addressing* is a gerund (a verb plus *-ing*, functioning as a noun). In the second sentence, *addressing* is a participle (a verb plus *-ing*, functioning as an adjective). In the last sentence, *addressing* is a verb (showing action).

Though not common, gerunds can occasionally create new compound verbs. Take for example the compound gerunds bar-tending or baby-sitting. These gerunds are composed of two parts, "bar" "tending" and "baby" "sitting." You could also divide these gerunds as "bartend" plus "-ing," and "babysit" plus "-ing." Since "-ing" is a suffix for verbs, "bartend" and "babysit" must be verbs. After all, *Paul can bartend on Friday nights*, and *Frannie can babysit next week*, so we have gerunds that have become new verbs. This process is called reanalysis, and while not very common does sometimes occur.

INFINITIVES

A Verb Plus "To"

The good news is that infinitives are easy to spot—usually. Infinitives are composed of *to* plus a verb (e.g., *to go, to carry*). Most often infinitives are used as nouns, but sometimes they crop up as adjectives or adverbs.

> *"I want to go home!" cried the youngster.*

To go is an infinitive acting as a noun.

> *We come to bury Caesar.*

To bury is an infinitive that acts as an adverb; it tells why we came.

> *Harry was the first guy in our crowd to marry.*

To marry is an infinitive that acts as an adjective; it describes *guy*. Now for the bad news. Sometimes the *to* part of an infinitive is omitted.

> *"Please help me mow the lawn," Arthur said to his wife.*

That sentence means the same as

> *"Please help me to mow the lawn . . . "*

Once you get used to looking at sentences in this way, you'll find that recognizing infinitives without the *to* will become automatic.

Many years ago grammarians decided that splitting an infinitive (that is, inserting a word—an adverb, to be exact—between *to* and the verb, as in *to plainly see* and *to hastily wed*) was wrong. Thankfully, that rule has gone by the wayside for all but the stuffiest editors.

Grammar Facts

Interestingly there was never an official grammar "rule" against split infinitives. The 1864 text *The Queen's English* said that there was "no good reason" to split infinitives but never actually said that they were incorrect. Other grammar texts through the years have hinted that split infinitives were "ugly" but again the writers never went so far as to say that splitting an infinitive was wrong.

Why was the "no split infinitive" rule created in the first place? In the days when the study of Latin was a mandatory part of the curriculum in many schools, rules of Latin grammar often affected rules of English grammar. Since a Latin infinitive is written as one word, it can't be split; therefore, grammarians said, the English infinitive should never be split either.

Look at the following sentence (with a split infinitive):

Georgia needed to better understand the rules of English grammar.

Now look at this sentence:

To really understand split infinitives, look at their construction.

That sentence constructed without using a split infinitive would be worded like this:

To understand really split infinitives, look at their construction.
or
Really to understand split infinitives, look at their construction.

Those don't do justice to the meaning of the sentence, do they? But now take a look at a sentence like this:

You're usually safe to make the split.

In that instance, if you split the infinitive, you'd end up with a sentence like this:

You're safe to usually make the split.
or
You're safe to make usually the split.

Neither of those sounds right, either. Better to leave the infinitive whole in that case. The moral of the story here is that you have to let your ear tell you if a split infinitive works. If it does, then by all means use it; if not, leave the infinitive alone.

SUBJECTS AND PREDICATES

The Parts of a Sentence

As you probably know, a sentence can be very short or very long. By definition, a sentence must have the following: (1) a predicate (usually called a verb), (2) the subject of that verb, and (3) words that form a complete thought. The complete subject is the person, place, or thing that the sentence is about, along with all the words that modify it. The complete predicate is what the person, place, or thing is doing, or what condition it is in.

> *Complete Subject*   *Complete Predicate (Verb)*
> *The elderly, white-haired gentleman walked quickly down the hallway.*

The simple subject of a sentence is the fundamental part of the complete subject—the main noun(s) and pronoun(s) in the complete subject. In the previous example, the simple subject is *gentleman*.

The simple predicate (verb) of a sentence is the fundamental part of the complete predicate—the verb(s) in the complete predicate. In the previous example, the simple predicate is *walked*.

Grammar Facts

Sometimes a word or phrase will come between the simple subject and the simple predicate. You will need to decide whether the phrase describes the subject or predicate.

> Alissa Truman, the drama club president, will be directing the play.
> (the drama club president describes Alissa)

> My little brother later explained who broke the picture.
> (later tells when he explained)

A sentence may also have compound subjects and predicates.

The elderly, white-haired gentleman and his wife walked quickly down the hallway.

This sentence has a compound subject: *gentleman* and *wife*.

The elderly, white-haired gentleman walked quickly down the hallway and then paused to speak to me.

This sentence has a compound verb: *walked* and *paused*.

The elderly, white-haired gentleman and his wife walked quickly down the hallway and then paused to speak to me.

This sentence has a compound subject—*gentleman* and *wife*—and a compound verb—*walked* and *paused*.

If you have trouble locating the subject of a sentence, find the verb and then ask *who* or *what* did the verb. Read this sentence:

After a tiring morning at the gym, Justin fell onto the floor in exhaustion.

The verb is *fell*. If you ask, "Who or what fell?" you answer *Justin*, which is the subject.

Remember that the subject of a sentence is never in a prepositional phrase. If the sentence is a question, the subject sometimes appears after the verb. To find the subject, turn the question around so that it resembles a declarative sentence. Then proceed in the normal way. Look at this sentence:

What is Willa going to do with that leftover sandwich?

Now, turn the wording around so that you have:

Willa is going to do what with that leftover sandwich?

Willa answers the *who?* or *what?* question about the verb *is going*. Finding the subject of a sentence helps you use verbs and pronouns correctly.

Grammar Facts

Some imperative sentences written in the second person are called "you understood" sentences. You know the subject of the sentence is *you*, even though *you* isn't spoken or written. Look at this sentence:

Go get me some lemonade.

You understand that the meaning is "You go get me some lemonade."

COMPLEMENTS

Requirements for Meaning

Although some sentences are complete with only a subject and a predicate, many others need something else to complete their meaning. These additional parts of a sentence are called complements, and English has five types: direct object, object complement, indirect object, predicate adjective, and predicate nominative. Predicate adjectives and predicate nominatives are considered subject complements.

DIRECT OBJECTS

One type of complement used with a transitive verb is a direct object: the word or words that receive the action of the verb. Direct objects are nouns (usually), pronouns (sometimes), or noun clauses (rarely). You can find a direct object by applying this formula:

1. First, find the subject of the sentence.
2. Second, find the verb, and make sure it's transitive.
3. Third, say the subject and predicate, and then ask *whom?* or *what?* If a word answers either of those questions, it's a direct object.

All of this sounds more complicated than it is. Look at this sentence:

The little boy constantly dribbled the basketball in the outdoor playground.

You can find the subject *(boy)* and the verb *(dribbled)*, so all you do is say *boy dribbled whom or what?* The word that answers that question *(basketball)* is the direct object. Easy enough, huh?

OBJECT COMPLEMENTS

Another kind of complement used with a transitive verb is an object (objective) complement; it elaborates on or gives a fuller meaning to a direct object. Object complements can be nouns, pronouns, or adjectives. Take a look at this sentence:

Helen and Ruth asked their sister Marie for a ride home.

In this sentence the direct object is *Marie* (Helen and Ruth asked whom or what? *Marie*), and the noun *sister* is the object complement. Object complements that act in this way—that is, they elaborate on the direct object—are nouns or pronouns.

Grammar Facts

In order for a sentence to have an indirect object, *to* or *for* must be implied, not stated. If either of those words is stated, then you have a prepositional phrase, not an indirect object.

Bob and Sara Payne made us a spaghetti dinner.

When you ask *Bob and Sara Payne made for whom?* the answer is *us. Us* is an indirect object.

Bob and Sara Payne made a spaghetti dinner for us.

Since *for* is in the sentence, *for us* is a prepositional phrase, not an indirect object.

Object complements can also be adjectives. Look at this sentence:

On a whim, both George and Lucy painted their fingernails blue.

In this sentence the direct object is *fingernails* (both painted whom or what? *fingernails*), and the adjective *blue* is the object complement. Object complements that act in this way—that is, they describe the direct object—are adjectives.

INDIRECT OBJECTS

The third type of complement used with a transitive verb is an indirect object. It comes before a direct object and answers the question *to whom?* or *for whom?* after the subject and verb. An easy formula for finding an indirect object is this:

1. First, find the subject of the sentence.
2. Second, find the transitive verb.
3. Third, say the subject and the predicate, and then ask *to whom?* or *for whom?* If a word answers that question, it's an indirect object.

Look at this example:

Drew reluctantly gave Courtney the keys to his new car.

In this sentence, the subject is *Drew* and the verb is *gave*. Using the formula of asking *to whom?* or *for whom?* after the subject and verb, you would say *Drew gave to whom?* The answer is *Courtney*.

SUBJECT COMPLEMENTS

Other kinds of complements, called subject complements, are used only with linking verbs. (Linking verbs, you'll remember, are all forms of *be* and, in certain situations, *appear, become, feel, grow, look, remain, smell, sound, stay,* and *taste*.) Subject complements do just what their name implies—they complete (give you more information about) the subject. Predicate adjectives and predicate nominatives are the two types of subject complements.

Predicate Adjectives

A predicate adjective is an adjective that comes after a linking verb and describes the subject of the sentence. To find a predicate adjective, apply this formula:

1. First, make sure the sentence has a linking verb.
2. Second, find the subject of the sentence.
3. Third, say the subject, say the linking verb, and then ask *what?* If a word answers the question *what?* and is an adjective, then you have a predicate adjective.

Here's an example of a predicate adjective:

Members of the Outlook Book Club are all intelligent.

Apply the formula for this sentence: (1) you know that *are* is a linking verb; (2) you find *members* as the subject of the sentence; (3) you say *members are what?* Since *intelligent* answers that question, and *intelligent* is an adjective, then you know that *intelligent* is a predicate adjective.

Predicate Nominatives

The other type of subject complement is the predicate nominative (predicate noun). It also comes after a linking verb and gives you more information about the subject. Here's a formula for finding a predicate nominative:

1. First, make sure the sentence has a linking verb.
2. Second, find the subject of the sentence.

3. Third, say the subject, say the linking verb, and then ask *who?* or *what?* If a word answers the questions *who?* or *what?* and is a noun or pronoun, you have a predicate nominative.

Grammar Facts

Any kind of complement may be compound.

I played basketball and football in high school.
(compound direct objects)

Lynne and Dick bought their dogs Bow and Wow new engraved collars.
(compound object complements)

Lucy is my aunt and my friend.
(compound predicate nominatives)

Look at this sentence:

That man over there is DeShawn.

Apply the formula for this sentence: (1) you know that *is* is a linking verb; (2) you find *man* as the subject of the sentence; (3) you say *man is who?* Since *DeShawn* answers that question, and *DeShawn* is a noun (it names a person), then you know that *DeShawn* is a predicate nominative.

Chapter 7

Tenses and Forms

Verb tenses are an attribute of verbs that tell us about time. Without giving it a second thought, you probably use certain tenses to express particular time periods. There are three basic times when verbs can take place—the past, the present, and the future. Of course, as with most grammatical subjects there are always complications. This chapter will take you through both simple and irregular verb (those that have unpredictable forms) tenses. This chapter will iron out all the complexities of the different verb forms for you so that choosing different tenses will never again make you, well, tense. You'll also learn about verb moods, which show the writer's attitude, and comparisons, which show how one thing compares to another.

VERB TENSES

Let's Talk Tense

English verbs are divided into three main tenses, all of which relate to time: present, past, and future. Each main tense is also subdivided into other categories: simple tense, progressive tense, perfect tense, and perfect progressive tense. These subcategories differentiate when a particular action has been done (or is being done or will be done). Clear as mud? Take a look at this chart:

	SIMPLE*	PROGRESSIVE**	PERFECT***	PERFECT PROGRESSIVE****
PRESENT	hide	am/is/are hiding	have/has hidden	have/has been hiding
PAST	hid	was/were hiding	had hidden	had been hiding
FUTURE	will/shall hide	will be hiding	will have hidden	will have been hiding

*Indicates action that is usual or is repeated
**Indicates action that is ongoing
***Indicates action that is completed
****Indicates ongoing action that will be completed at some definite time

Each of these tenses signals the time something is done, will be done, or has been done relative to when it's being written or spoken about. You still don't quite get the whole thing? Don't worry; all will be cleared up in the next few pages, starting with explanations for each of the tenses. To begin our discussion, why don't we start with a little joke:

Professor Reynolds says to her student, "Conjugate the verb 'to walk' in the simple present tense."

The student says, "I walk. You walk. He . . . "
Interrupting, Professor Reynolds says, "More quickly, please."
The student replies, "I run. You run. . . . "

THE SIMPLE TENSE

The *simple present tense* tells an action that is usual or repeated:

I hide from the stalker.

Looked at in a different way, the simple present tense relates actions that happen often or that state a fact or opinion.

To make sure they're using the correct verb form for the present tense, some writers find it helpful to mentally begin the sentence with the word *today*:

Today I hide from the stalker.

The *simple past tense* tells an action that began and ended in the past:

I hid from the stalker.

To make sure they're using the correct verb form for the past tense, some writers find it helpful to mentally begin the sentence with the word *yesterday*:

Yesterday I hid from the stalker.

The *simple future tense* tells an upcoming action that will occur:

I will hide from the stalker.

To make sure they're using the correct verb form for the future tense, some writers find it helpful to mentally begin the sentence with the word *tomorrow*:

Tomorrow I will hide from the stalker.

That's simple enough, isn't it? It's the simple present tense. After this, though, the explanations of the other tenses get a little tricky.

Grammar Facts

Some verbs, called stative verbs, aren't used in certain tenses because they describe a state of being rather than an action. These verbs usually relate to thoughts, emotions, senses, or relationships. These verbs usually are not used with the *–ing* in progressive tenses. For example:

Do you *recognize* her, she went to high school with you.

Karen *appreciated* the work you did on the fundraiser.

THE PROGRESSIVE TENSE

Use the *present progressive tense* to show an action that's in progress at the time the statement is written:

I am hiding from the stalker today.

Present progressive verbs are always formed by using *am*, *is*, or *are* and adding *-ing* to the verb. Use the *past progressive tense* to show an action that was going on at some particular time in the past:

I was hiding from the stalker yesterday.

Past progressive verbs are always formed by using *was* or *were* and adding *-ing* to the verb. Use the *future progressive tense* to show an action that's continuous and that will occur in the future:

I will be hiding from the stalker tomorrow.

Future progressive verbs are always formed by using *will be* or *shall be* and adding *-ing* to the verb.

THE PERFECT TENSE

Use the *present perfect tense* to convey action that happened sometime in the past or that started in the past but is ongoing in the present:

I have hidden from the stalker for more than five years.

Present perfect verbs are always formed by using *has* or *have* and the past participle form of the verb. Use the *past perfect tense* to indicate past action that occurred prior to another past action:

I had hidden from the stalker for more than five years before I entered the Witness Protection Program.

Past perfect verbs are always formed by using *had* and the past participle form of the verb. Use the *future perfect tense* to illustrate future action that will occur before some other action:

I will have hidden from the stalker for more than five years before entering the Witness Protection Program.

Future perfect verbs are always formed by using *will have* and the past participle form of the verb.

PARTICULARS OF THE PERFECT
PROGRESSIVE TENSE

Use the *present perfect progressive* to illustrate an action repeated over a period of time in the past, continuing in the present, and possibly carrying on in the future:

For the past five years, I have been hiding from the stalker.

Present perfect progressive verbs are always formed by using *has been* or *have been* and adding *-ing* to the verb.

Use the *past perfect progressive* to illustrate a past continuous action that was completed before some other past action:

Before I entered the Witness Protection Program, I had been hiding from the stalker for more than five years.

Past perfect progressive verbs are always formed by using *had been* and adding *-ing* to the verb.

Use the *future perfect progressive* to illustrate a future continuous action that will be completed before some future time:

Next month I will have been hiding from the stalker for five years.

Future perfect progressive verbs are always formed by using *will have been* and adding *-ing* to the verb.

IRREGULAR VERBS

Some Verbs Just Don't Fit In

The good news is that most English verbs form their past and past participle by adding -d or -ed to the base form of the verb (the form you'd find listed first in the dictionary). These are called regular verbs.

The bad news is that English has a number of verb forms that aren't formed in that way; some people call them "those %*#@^ verbs," but usually they're called irregular verbs (clever, huh?). Here's a list of often-used irregular English verbs.

VERBS THAT TAKE AN IRREGULAR FORM

BASE (INFINITIVE)	SIMPLE PAST	PAST PARTICIPLE
abide	abode/abided	abode/abided
arise	arose	arisen
awake	awoke/awaked	awaked/awoken
be	was, were	been
beat	beat	beaten/beat
become	became	become
begin	began	begun
bend	bent	bent
bet	bet/betted	bet/betted
bid	bade/bid	bidden/bid
bind	bound	bound
bite	bit	bitten/bit
bleed	bled	bled
blow	blew	blown
break	broke	broken

VERBS THAT TAKE AN IRREGULAR FORM

BASE (INFINITIVE)	SIMPLE PAST	PAST PARTICIPLE
breed	bred	bred
bring	brought	brought
build	built	built
burn	burned/burnt	burned/burnt
buy	bought	bought
catch	caught	caught
choose	chose	chosen
cling	clung	clung
come	came	come
creep	crept	crept
dig	dug	dug
dive	dived/dove	dived
do	did	done
draw	drew	drawn
dream	dreamed/dreamt	dreamed/dreamt
drink	drank	drunk
drive	drove	driven
eat	ate	eaten
fall	fell	fallen
feed	fed	fed
feel	felt	felt
fight	fought	fought
find	found	found
fit	fitted/fit	fit
flee	fled	fled

VERBS THAT TAKE AN IRREGULAR FORM

BASE (INFINITIVE)	SIMPLE PAST	PAST PARTICIPLE
fling	flung	flung
fly	flew	flown
forsake	forsook	forsaken
freeze	froze	frozen
get	got	gotten/got
give	gave	given
go	went	gone
grind	ground	ground
grow	grew	grown
hang (to suspend)	hung	hung
has	had	had
have	had	had
hear	heard	heard
hide	hid	hidden/hid
hit	hit	hit
hold	held	held
hurt	hurt	hurt
input	input	input
inset	inset	inset
interbreed	interbred	interbred
keep	kept	kept
kneel	knelt/kneeled	knelt/kneeled
knit	knit/knitted	knit/knitted
know	knew	known
lay	laid	laid

VERBS THAT TAKE AN IRREGULAR FORM

BASE (INFINITIVE)	SIMPLE PAST	PAST PARTICIPLE
lead	led	led
lean	leaned	leaned
leap	leaped/leapt	leaped/leapt
learn	learned/learnt	learned/learnt
leave	left	left
lend	lent	lent
lie (to rest or recline)	lay	lain
light	lighted/lit	lighted/lit
lose	lost	lost
make	made	made
mean	meant	meant
meet	met	met
mistake	mistook	mistaken
mow	mowed	mowed/mown
pay	paid	paid
plead	pleaded/pled	pleaded/pled
prove	proved/proven	proved/proven
quit	quit/quitted	quit/quitted
read	read	read
ring	rang	rung
rise	rose	risen
run	ran	run
say	said	said
see	saw	seen
sell	sold	sold

VERBS THAT TAKE AN IRREGULAR FORM

BASE (INFINITIVE)	SIMPLE PAST	PAST PARTICIPLE
send	sent	sent
shoot	shot	shot
show	showed	shown/showed
sing	sang/sung	sung
sink	sank/sunk	sunk
sit	sat	sat
sleep	slept	slept
slide	slid	slid
smell	smelled/smelt	smelled/smelt
smite	smote	smitten/smote
sow	sowed	sown/sowed
speak	spoke	spoken
speed	sped/speeded	sped/speeded
spell	spelled/spelt	spelled/spelt
spend	spent	spent
spill	spilled/spilt	spilled/spilt
spin	spun	spun
spit	spat/spit	spat/spit
split	split	split
spoil	spoiled/spoilt	spoiled/spoilt
spring	sprang/sprung	sprung
stand	stood	stood
steal	stole	stolen
stick	stuck	stuck
sting	stung	stung

VERBS THAT TAKE AN IRREGULAR FORM

BASE (INFINITIVE)	SIMPLE PAST	PAST PARTICIPLE
stink	stank/stunk	stunk
strew	strewed	strewn/strewed
stride	strode	stridden
strike	struck	struck/stricken
string	strung	strung
strive	strove	striven/strived
swear	swore	sworn
sweep	swept	swept
swell	swelled	swelled/swollen
swim	swam	swum
swing	swung	swung
take	took	taken
teach	taught	taught
tear	tore	torn
tell	told	told
think	thought	thought
throw	threw	thrown
tread	trod	trodden/trod
understand	understood	understood
wake	woke/waked	waked/woken
wear	wore	worn
weave	wove	woven
wed	wedded	wed/wedded
weep	wept	wept
wet	wet/wetted	wet/wetted

GRAMMAR 101

VERBS THAT TAKE AN IRREGULAR FORM

BASE (INFINITIVE)	SIMPLE PAST	PAST PARTICIPLE
win	won	won
wind	wound	wound
wring	wrung	wrung

Just to keep you on your toes, two verbs—*hang and lie*—may be regular or irregular, depending on their meaning in the sentence. If *hang* means *to use a noose*, it's a regular verb. If it means *to affix to a wall*, it's irregular. For example:

Prison officials discovered a picture the hanged man's mother had hung in his cell.

If *lie* means *to tell a falsehood*, it's a regular verb. If it means *to rest or recline*, it's irregular. Here's an example:

Dave lay on the beach and lied when he phoned in sick.

Grammar Facts

There are almost 200 irregular verbs in normal use and as you can see from the previous table they are often some of the most frequently used verbs in English. Most irregular verbs are derived from Old English whereas new verbs—words borrowed from other languages or those that are nouns used as verbs (such as *to google)*—tend to be regular.

VERB MOODS

How Are You Feeling?

In addition to tenses, English verbs are divided into moods, which show the writer's attitude toward what he or she is saying. The first two moods, indicative and imperative, aren't confusing at all, and, fortunately, they're used far more frequently than the third mood, subjunctive.

Almost all verbs are used in the indicative mood, which means that the verb's sentence states a fact or an actuality. All of these sentences are in the indicative mood:

> *I'll be seeing you later on tonight.*
> *Wear whatever you want.*
> *You look nice in anything.*
> *We're all casual dressers, so don't worry about your attire.*

Verbs used in the imperative mood are in sentences that make requests or give a command. All of these sentences are in the imperative mood:

> *Please give me the phone.*
> *Give it to me right now!*
> *Give it to me—or else!*

The subjunctive mood is the one that speakers and writers sometimes have problems with. Fortunately, it's used with only two verbs (*be* and *were*), and in modern English, it's used in only two kinds of sentences:

1. Statements that are contrary to fact (providing they begin with *if* or *unless*), improbable, or doubtful

2. Statements that express a wish, a request or recommendation, an urgent appeal, or a demand

The following are verb forms used in the subjunctive mood:

PRESENT SUBJUNCTIVE

SINGULAR	PLURAL
(if) I be	(if) we be
(if) you be	(if) you be
(if) he/she/it be	(if) they be

PAST SUBJUNCTIVE

SINGULAR	PLURAL
(if) I were	(if) we were
(if) you were	(if) you were
(if) he/she/it were	(if) they were

Grammar Facts

Some grammarians also mention the conditional and infinitive moods. A conditional mood shows under what conditions something might happen. This verb mood uses the words *might*, *could*, and *would*. For example:

I might be able to go to the concert if I can scrape up some cash.

The infinitive mood expresses action but doesn't have a subject because the verb is not being used as a verb in the sentence. For example:

He came to see you. (*to see you* is used as an adverb here)

Here is an example:

It's important that everybody be [not is] at the meeting.

This is a wish or request—a strong request, at that.

If I were in your position, I would do the same.

I am not in your position, so the statement is contrary to fact.

Some verbs that often attract the subjunctive mood are: ask, command, demand, insist, order, recommend, suggest, and wish. Additionally some adjectives attract the subjunctive mood including: crucial, essential, important, imperative, and necessary.

MAKING COMPARISONS

How Does It Measure Up?

Sometimes you need to show how something compares with or measures up to something else. Say, for example, you and your family enjoy watching horror movies. You may want to report about a new scary movie you've seen, deciding whether it's *scarier* than another one you've all recently watched together or perhaps even the *scariest* movie you've ever seen. A scary movie can become a *scarier* movie if it's compared to another one, or it can become the *scariest* movie if it's compared to several others.

In writing comparisons, you use one of three different forms (called degrees) of adjectives and adverbs:

- The positive degree simply makes a statement about a person, place, or thing.
- The comparative degree compares two (but only two) people, places, or things.
- The superlative degree compares more than two people, places, or things.

POSITIVE	COMPARATIVE	SUPERLATIVE
blue	bluer	bluest
happy	happier	happiest
tall	taller	tallest

Here are rules to help you form the comparative and superlative:

- **Rule 1.** One-syllable adjectives and adverbs usually form their comparative form by adding *-er* and their superlative form by adding *-est* (see the examples *tall* and *blue* in the table).

- **Rule 2.** Adjectives of more than two syllables and adverbs ending in *-ly* usually form comparative forms by using *more* (or *less*) and superlative forms by using *most* (or *least*).

POSITIVE	COMPARATIVE	SUPERLATIVE
comfortable	more comfortable	most comfortable
qualified	less qualified	least qualified

- **Rule 3.** Confusion sometimes crops up in forming comparisons of words of two syllables only. Here's the rub: Sometimes two-syllable words use the *-er*, *-est* forms, and sometimes they use the *more*, *most* (or *less*, *least*) forms. You knew there had to be some complications in there somewhere, didn't you?

POSITIVE	COMPARATIVE	SUPERLATIVE
sleepy	sleepier	sleepiest
tiring	more tiring	most tiring

So how do you know whether to use the *-er*, *-est* form or the *more*, *most* form? You have to use a dictionary (a large dictionary, not a paperback one) if you're not sure. If no comparative or superlative forms are listed in the dictionary, use the *more*, *most* form.

Grammar Rules

Some adjectives don't have degrees. There is only one level of these adjectives. For example the word *fatal*. Something can not be *more fatal*, it either *is* fatal or it *is not*. Other examples include: *entire*, *final*, *half*, *main*, and *pregnant*.

Did you happen to notice the word *usually* in the first two rules? It's there because English has some exceptions to the rules. The good news is that the exceptions are few. Among them are:

POSITIVE	COMPARATIVE	SUPERLATIVE
bad	worse	worst
far	farther/further	farthest/furthest
little	littler/less/lesser	littlest/least
many	more	most
old (persons)	elder	eldest

One common mistake in both writing and speaking is to use the superlative form when the comparative should be used. If you're comparing two persons, places, or things, you use only the comparative form (not the superlative). Look at these sentences:

Of my two dogs, the cocker spaniel is the friendliest.
Tillie has two sons; Charlie is the eldest and Herb is the youngest.

In both of those sentences, the comparison is between only two *(two dogs, two sons)*, so the sentences should be written with the comparative form *(friendlier, elder/younger)* instead of the superlative.

Another frequent mistake in comparisons is in going overboard—using both the *-er* and *more* or *-est* and *most* forms with the same noun, as in *the most tallest statue* or *a more happier child*. Remember that one form is the limit (and, of course, it has to be the correct form). In the examples, *most* and *more* need to be eliminated.

AVOIDING DOUBLE NEGATIVES

Two Wrongs Can Make a Right

When two negatives are used in a single clause, it is called a double negative. Double negative are usually used to stress denial or opposition, as in these examples:

After he had been laid off, Hal realized that he didn't need none of the luxuries he'd become accustomed to.

(*Didn't* and *none* are negatives. The sentence should be "After he had been laid off, Hal realized that he didn't need any of the luxuries he'd become accustomed to.")

That man was not doing nothing but just standing there!

(*Not* and *nothing* are negatives. The sentence should be "That man was not doing anything but just standing there!")

Allison wondered why Jason didn't call nobody when he became sick.

(*Didn't* and *nobody* are negatives. The sentence should be "Allison wondered why Jason didn't call anybody when he became sick.")

Mr. Fowler said he ain't got none of those apples that you want.

(*Ain't* and *none* are negatives—and you also know that *ain't* is considered nonstandard, don't you? The sentence should be "Mr. Fowler said he did not have any of those apples that you want.")

You'll often hear or read double negatives in colloquial speech:

You ain't heard nothin' yet!
Ike said he hadn't seen Betty nowhere.

Properly, these sentences should be "You haven't heard anything yet!" and "Ike said he hadn't seen Betty anywhere."

Grammar Facts

A litotes is a figure of speech that utilizes two negative terms in order to understate a certain fact. For example: "I would *not* say that he is an *unintelligent* man." So while both double negatives and litotes use two negative terms their purposes are different. A double negative creates a meaning the opposite of what it is supposed to mean, while a litotes is used to understate a fact and means exactly what it is supposed to mean. As such a litotes is an acceptable form of a double negative.

Double negative are usually not considered acceptable except in informal language but one exception to the rule comes if you intend a positive or lukewarm meaning. Read this sentence:

I was not unhappy with my recent raise.

The connotation in the double negatives (*not* and *unhappy*) tells readers that, while the writer wasn't unhappy, he or she wasn't exactly thrilled.

You may also use double negatives if you're using a phrase or clause for emphasis, as in this example:

"I will not take a bribe, not today, not tomorrow, not any time in my life," the politician cried.

And then of course there is the classic grammar double negative joke:

> *A linguistics professor was lecturing to his class one day. "In English," he said, "a double negative forms a positive. In some languages, such as Russian, a double negative is still a negative. However, there is no language wherein a double positive can form a negative."*
>
> *A voice from the back of the room piped up in reply, "Yeah, right."*

Chapter 8

Phrases, Clauses, and Sentence Structure

You have to crawl before you walk. In the first few chapters, you were crawling through grammar—re-examining punctuation, parts of speech, and parts of a sentence. Now you can progress to walking—putting punctuation and words together in more complex forms.

FUNDAMENTAL PHRASES

Multiple Words with One Function

A phrase is a group of words that acts as a particular part of speech or part of a sentence but doesn't have a verb and its subject. The most common type of phrase is the prepositional phrase.

A prepositional phrase is a group of words that begins with a preposition and ends with a noun or pronoun (the object of the preposition). Here are a few examples:

during the terrible storm
after Tom and Norma's dinner
through the open doorway
for Rufie and Phyllis

In a sentence, prepositional phrases act as adjectives (they describe nouns or pronouns; they also answer the question *which one?* or *what kind of?*) or adverbs (they describe verbs, adjectives, or other adverbs; they also answer the question *when? where? how? why? to what extent?* or *under what condition?*).

Grammar Facts

Here are some basic prepositional phrases: at home (*at* is the preposition, *home* is the noun); in time (*in* is the preposition, *time* is the noun); with me (*with* is the preposition, *me* is the pronoun); from Ryan (*from* is the preposition, *Ryan* is the noun).

ADJECTIVE PHRASES

Adjective phrase: *Several friends from my job are getting together tonight.*

From my job is a prepositional phrase that acts as an adjective. It's an adjective phrase because it modifies or describes the noun *friends*. If you look at it in another way, *from my job* is an adjective phrase because it answers the question *which ones?* An adjective phrase is almost always placed right after the word or words it modifies.

ADVERB PHRASES

Adverb phrase: *Tom and Debbie will meet at Wolf's Restaurant later tonight.*

At Wolf's Restaurant is a prepositional phrase that acts as an adverb. It's an adverb phrase because it modifies or describes the verb *meet*. If you look at it in another way, *at Wolf's Restaurant* is an adverb phrase because it answers the question *where?*

PARTICIPIAL PHRASES

Another type of phrase is the participial phrase, which is composed of a participle and any words that modify it or are related to it. A participle, you remember, is a word formed from a verb plus an ending. A participle acts as an adjective; that is, it describes a noun or pronoun in your sentence. Present participles always end in *-ing*; past participles usually end in *-d* or *–ed*, but English has many exceptions.

For example:

Fleeing from the sudden storm, picnickers Leslie and Dino sought refuge in the shelter house at the park.

Fleeing is a present participle; it has a verb *flee* plus *-ing*, and it describes the noun *picnickers*. *Fleeing* and the words that go with it—*from the sudden storm*—make up the participial phrase.

A third type of phrase is the gerund phrase, which is a gerund and any words that modify it or are related to it in your sentence. Remember that a gerund is a word that is formed from a verb plus *-ing*. Since a gerund acts as a noun, it can be a subject or an object. Look at this sentence:

Singing the night away helped Charles and Catherine forget their troubles.

Singing is a gerund; it's composed of the verb *sing* plus *-ing*. In this sentence, it acts as the subject. *Singing* and the words that go with it—*the night away*—make up the gerund phrase.

INFINITIVE PHRASES

A fourth type of phrase is the infinitive phrase, which is an infinitive and any words that modify it. An infinitive, you know, is *to* plus a verb. An infinitive can act as several parts of speech—a noun, an adjective, or an adverb. For example:

"To go home right now is my only wish," sighed the tired mother.

To go is an infinitive; it's composed of *to* plus the verb *go*. In this sentence, it acts as the subject of the sentence. The infinitive *To go* and the word that goes with it—*home*—make up the infinitive phrase.

APPOSITIVE PHRASES

The final type of phrase is an appositive phrase, which is an appositive and any words that modify it or are related to it. An appositive is a noun (usually) or pronoun (rarely) that gives details or identifies another noun or pronoun. Here's an example:

My favorite book, a dog-eared copy of To Kill a Mockingbird, *has accompanied me on many vacations.*

Copy is an appositive that refers to *book*. In this sentence, *copy* and the words that go with it—*a dog-eared*—make up the appositive phrase: *a dog-eared copy of* To Kill a Mockingbird.

CLAUSES

A More Complex Phrase

A clause is just a notch more complicated than a phrase. Like a phrase, a clause is used as a particular part of speech or part of a sentence; however, unlike a phrase, a clause has a verb and its subject. Independent and subordinate are the two main types of clauses.

The Declaration of Independent Clauses

An independent (main) clause is a group of words that has a verb and its subject. Also, this group of words could stand alone as a sentence; that is, the words could make sense if they were by themselves. Here's an example:

The index cards fell to the floor.

This is one independent clause. It has a subject *(cards)* and a verb *(fell)*, and it stands alone as a sentence. Now, look at this sentence:

The index cards scattered on the floor, and Ora Lou and Gene had to pick them all up.

This sentence has two independent clauses. The first—*the index cards scattered on the floor*—has a subject *cards* and a verb *scattered*; it could stand alone as a sentence. The second—*Ora Lou and Gene had to pick them all up*—has subjects (*Ora Lou* and *Gene*) and a verb (*had*); it also could stand alone as a sentence.

Grammar Facts

Independent clauses joined by *and*, *but*, *for*, *or*, *nor*, *so*, or *yet* are separated by a comma. Other independent clauses are separated by a semicolon.

Now look:

Ora Lou and Gene had just alphabetized the index cards when the cards fell on the floor and scattered everywhere.

The independent clause in this sentence is *Ora Lou and Gene had just alphabetized the index cards.* Although the rest of the sentence—*when the cards fell on the floor and scattered everywhere*—has a subject (*cards*) and verbs (*fell* and *scattered*), it can't stand alone as a complete thought; because of this, it's not an independent clause.

SUBORDINATE CLAUSES

A subordinate (dependent) clause has a verb and its subject, but it can't stand alone as a sentence. When you read the words of a subordinate clause, you can see a subject and a verb but the words don't make sense by themselves. In order for a subordinate clause to make sense, it has to be attached to another part (to some independent clause) of the sentence. A subordinate clause usually begins with a subordinating conjunction or a relative pronoun. Look at the last example in the discussion about independent clauses:

Ora Lou and Gene had just alphabetized the index cards when the cards fell on the floor and scattered everywhere.

In this sentence, *when the cards fell on the floor and scattered everywhere* is a subordinate clause. It has a subject *cards* and verbs *fell* and *scattered.* But read the words alone:

when the cards fell on the floor and scattered everywhere

So, what about them? What happened next? If the terminology of clauses seems complicated, think of the relationship this way: Since a subordinate clause can't stand alone, it's secondary (subordinate) to the main clause of the sentence. Or, a subordinate clause relies (is dependent) on another clause (an independent clause) that's in the same sentence.

English has three types of subordinate clauses, and each acts in a different way in a sentence.

Adjective Clauses

An adjective clause is a subordinate clause that acts as an adjective; it modifies or describes a noun or pronoun. Looked at a different way, an adjective clause answers *which one?* or *what kind of?* An adjective clause is sometimes called a relative clause because relative pronouns *(who, whose, whom, which,* and *that)* often begin adjective clauses and relate the clause to the person, place, or thing that they describe.

That man, whom I knew in high school, walked right by as if he'd never met me.

Whom I knew in high school is an adjective clause. It has a verb *(knew)* and its subject *(I),* and it can't stand alone as a sentence—that's what makes it a subordinate clause. It's an adjective clause because it describes the noun *man;* in addition, it answers the question *which one?* about *man.*

Careful! Just to confuse you, sometimes an adjective clause has *that* deleted from it.

The new CD that Bill and Becky Brown want has not yet been released.

The new CD Bill and Becky Brown want has not yet been released.

Grammar Facts

Because an adjective clause modifies a noun, it can modify a subject, direct object, indirect object, predicate nominative, or object of a preposition.

Noun Clauses

A noun clause is a subordinate clause that acts as a noun; it can be the subject, predicate nominative, appositive, object of a verb, or object of a preposition. A noun clause answers *who? whom?* or *what?*

Kevin, Lynda, and Mike couldn't believe what they heard at the library.

What they heard at the library is a noun clause. It has a subject (*they*) and a verb (*heard*) and it can't stand alone as a sentence, so it's some type of subordinate clause. Because it's the direct object of *couldn't believe* (and therefore functions in the sentence as a noun), it's a noun clause.

Grammar Facts

A noun clause is often introduced by *if, how, that, what, whatever, when, where, whether, which, who, whoever, whom, whomever, whose,* or *why.*

Adverb Clauses

An adverb clause is a subordinate clause that acts as an adverb; it can modify or describe a verb, an adjective, or another adverb. Looked at in a different way, an adverb clause answers *when? where? how? why? to what extent? with what goal or result?* or *under what condition or circumstances?* An adverb clause is introduced by a subordinating conjunction, such as *after, although, as (if), because, once, until,* and *while.*

Mr. Kasenow visited Kim because he was attracted to her.

Because he was attracted to her is an adverb clause. It has a subject (*he*) and a verb (*was attracted*). It can't stand alone as a sentence, so it's some type of subordinate clause. Because it modifies the verb *visited*, it's an adverb clause.

Remember to use a comma after an introductory adverb clause, as in this example:

Whenever he came to visit, Mr. Kasenow brought Kim a box of candy.

Using Clauses

By eliminating the noun or pronoun and changing the verb, you can change clauses into phrases; in the same vein, you can add a subject and verb to a phrase and create a clause. Why would you want to change clauses into phrases (or vice versa)? After you've written a paragraph, you might notice that you've used the same style in several sentences, and because of that your writing seems monotonous or singsongy. Reconstructing your sentences by changing clauses and phrases might help eliminate that effect and make your paragraph livelier. Notice the difference here:

Adjective clause: The green van that is on the used car lot caught my eye.

Adjective phrase: The green van on the used car lot caught my eye.

By the same token, you can convert a subordinate clause into an independent clause by adding a few words.

RESTRICTIVE AND NONRESTRICTIVE CLAUSES

Clauses are also divided in another way, depending on whether they're necessary in a sentence. A restrictive clause (essential clause or a defining clause) is necessary to the basic meaning of the sentence; a nonrestrictive clause (nonessential clause or nondefining clause) can be eliminated from the sentence without changing its basic meaning.

The car that Donald and Shirley Wathen had just purchased was stolen.

The car, which was stolen last Saturday, has been found.

In the first example, the clause *that Donald and Shirley Wathen had just purchased* is necessary to complete the meaning of the sentence. In the second example, including the clause *which was stolen last Saturday* isn't necessary in order to understand what the sentence says. In this instance, the clause is merely extra information.

Grammar Facts

What's the difference between a phrase and a clause? A clause has a verb and its subject; a phrase doesn't.

Notice in the preceding examples the word *that* introduces restrictive clauses, and *which* introduces nonrestrictive clauses. In general, note how particular words introduce different types of clauses. In determining parts of speech, look at the way the word is used in the sentence; in determining a type of clause, look at the way the clause is used in the sentence.

CONSTRUCTING SENTENCES

What's Your Type?

Now that you've examined words, phrases, and clauses, you can put them all together and make sentences. Or can you? The truth is, you need a few additional facts. Grammarians get technical with sentences, just as they do with the parts that make up the sentences. Sentences are classified in both the way they're arranged (this is called sentence type) and in the way they function.

SURVEYING SENTENCE TYPES

You can determine the type of sentence by looking at *what kind* of clauses the sentence has and *how many* clauses the sentence has. Sentence types come in one of four categories: simple, compound, complex, and compound-complex.

A simple sentence has one independent clause and no subordinate clause:

The man on the dapple gray horse confidently rode into town.

This sentence has one subject *(man)* and one verb *(rode)*.

A simple sentence may have compound subjects or verbs, but it has only one complete thought (one independent or main clause).

A compound sentence has at least two independent clauses (two main clauses) but no subordinate clause (no dependent clause):

The man on the dapple gray horse confidently rode into town, and the townspeople began to fear for their lives.

This sentence has two independent clauses joined by *and*.

A complex sentence has one independent clause (main clause) and one or more subordinate clauses (dependent clauses):

Although he had been warned not to come, the man on the dapple gray horse confidently rode into town.

This sentence has one independent clause (*the man on the dapple gray horse confidently rode into town*) and one subordinate clause (*although he had been warned not to come*).

Using complex and compound-complex sentences helps to keep your writing from being monotonous. A compound-complex sentence has at least two independent clauses (main clauses) and one or more subordinate clauses (dependent clauses):

Although he had been warned not to come, the man on the dapple gray horse confidently rode into town, and the townspeople feared for their lives.

This sentence has one subordinate clause (*although he had been warned not to come*) and two independent clauses (*the man on the dapple gray horse confidently rode into town* and *the townspeople feared for their lives*).

Grammar Facts

Remember that independent clauses are joined by a comma plus one of the *boysfan* words *(but, or, yet, so, for, and,* or *nor)* or by a semicolon.

SENTENCE FUNCTIONS

Sentences function in four different ways; they can be declarative, interrogative, imperative, or exclamatory.

A declarative sentence makes a statement:

Tomorrow we can talk about our weekend plans.

An interrogative sentence asks a question:

Do you think we can talk about our weekend plans tomorrow?

Grammar Facts

Sometimes you have a combination of sentence types.

I'll see you tomorrow, won't I?

The first part is a declarative sentence, and the second part is called a tag question.

An imperative sentence issues a command, makes a request, or gives instructions:

Come here so we can talk about our weekend plans.

An exclamatory sentence expresses strong emotion:

How I hope we can be together this weekend!

SUBJECT-VERB AGREEMENT

Disagreements Make for a Rocky Sentence

Do you ever notice some kind of incompatibility in your sentences? When you read your sentences, do you hear a jarring ring that tells you that something's wrong? The problem may be that you have disagreement between your subjects and verbs. To smooth out the situation, all you need to do is be sure that you follow the rule about subject-verb agreement: You must make verbs agree with their subjects in number and in person.

Okay, that's the rule, but what does it mean? The first part (*make the verb agree with its subject in number*) is just this simple: If you use a singular subject, you have to use a singular verb; if you use a plural subject, you have to use a plural verb. Nothing hard about that, is there?

Well, as you probably suspect, a number of situations can arise to make the rule tricky.

Grammar Facts

Titles of books, movies, and so on are always singular. It doesn't matter how long the title is or even if it sounds like a plural, it is always a singular entity and will take a singular verb. For example:

The Grapes of Wrath is a haunting tale.

Cars is a great movie for both boys and girls of any age.

The Tale of Despereaux: Being the Story of a Mouse, a Princess, Some Soup, and a Spool of Thread is an uplifting and sentimental story.

THE PROBLEM OF PREPOSITIONS

One problem comes with using the wrong word as your subject. To keep from making this mistake, remember this hint: Mentally disregard any prepositional phrases that come after the subject. Prepositional phrases will just distract you. Take a look at these sentences:

The tray of ice cubes (has, have) fallen on the kitchen floor.

Since you know to disregard the prepositional phrase *of ice cubes,* you then have:

The tray ~~of ice cubes~~ (has, have) fallen on the kitchen floor.

Now, you're left with the subject of the sentence (*tray*). Of course, you would say,

"The tray has fallen on the kitchen floor."

Look at another example:

Katie and Matt, along with their dog Pretzel, (was, were) walking down Hillcrest Boulevard.

Again, mentally cross off the prepositional phrase—no matter how long it is—and you have:

Katie and Matt, ~~along with their dog Pretzel~~, (was, were) walking down Hillcrest Boulevard.

You'd have no problem saying "Katie and Matt were walking down Hillcrest Boulevard," so that lets you know the correct verb to use.

PINPOINTING THE PRONOUNS

If an indefinite pronoun is the subject of your sentence, you have to look at the individual pronoun. Sometimes this is a snap, as with the plural pronouns that take a plural verb *(both, few, many, others, several)*. Look at these sentences:

*"Several scouts are [not **is**] in the stands at tonight's game,"* whispered the coach.

*A few of us want [not **wants**] to go camping this weekend.*

Just as some plural indefinite pronouns are easy to spot, so are some singular indefinite pronouns *(another, anybody, anyone, anything, each, either, everybody, everyone, everything, much, neither, no one, nobody, nothing, one, other, somebody, someone, something)*. The problem with indefinite pronouns is that a few of them are considered to be singular, even though they indicate a plural number *(e.g., each, everybody, everyone, everything)*. For example:

*Everybody is [not **are**] here, so we can start the trip.*

*No one is [not **are**] going to complain if you pick up the tab for tonight's meal.*

Now comes a tricky rule: Five pronouns *(all, any, most, none,* and *some)* sometimes take a singular verb and sometimes take a plural verb. How do you know which one to use? This is the time—the only time—you break the rule about disregarding the prepositional phrases. Take a look at these sentences:

*"Some of the money is [not **are**] missing!" cried the teller.*

*"Some of the people in the bank are [not **is**] the suspects,"* replied *the policeman.*

*Most of my coworkers were [not **was**] cleared of any suspicion.*

*Most of my jewelry is [not **are**] still missing.*

In each case, you have to look at the object of the preposition (*money, people, coworkers, jewelry*) to decide whether to use a singular or plural verb.

SEEKING SOLUTIONS TO SOME SPECIAL SITUATIONS

Here are some more oddities of English grammar (as if you haven't seen enough of them already):

The phrase *the only one of those* uses a singular verb; however, the phrase *one of those* uses a plural verb. (Is your head spinning?) Maybe these examples will help:

*The only one of those people I feel comfortable with is [not **are**] Vicki Brand.*

*Vicki Brand is one of those people who always listen [not **listens**] when I have a problem.*

If you have a sentence with *every* or *many a* before a word or group of words, use a singular verb. For example:

*Many a good man is [not **are**] trying to please his wife.*
*Every wife tries [not **try**] to help her husband understand.*

When the phrase *the number* is part of the subject of a sentence, it takes a singular verb. When the phrase *a number* is part of the subject, it takes a plural verb. Look at these sentences:

*The number of people who came to the concert is [not **are**] disappointing.*

*A number of people are [not **is**] at home watching the finals of the basketball tournament.*

When the phrase *more than one* is part of the subject, it takes a singular verb:

*More than one person is [not **are**] upset about the outcome of the election.*

Another time that subjects may be singular or plural is with collective nouns. Collective nouns (*cast, fleet,* or *gang*) name groups. Use a singular verb if you mean that the individual members of the group act or think together (they act as one unit). Use a plural verb if you mean that the individual members of the group act or think separately (they have different opinions or actions). For example:

The couple is renewing its donation of $50,000 for scholarships. (The two people were donating as a unit.)

The couple were cleared of the charges of embezzlement of $50,000. (The two were cleared separately.)

Still another problem with singular and plural verbs comes with expressions of amount. When the particular measurement or quantity (e.g., of time, money, weight, volume, food, or fractions) is considered as one unit or group, then use a singular verb:

*Ten dollars to see this movie is [not **are**] highway robbery!*

*"Five hours is [not **are**] too long to wait for this plane to take off,"*
complained the angry passenger.

*I would estimate that two-thirds of the snow has [not **have**]*
melted.

Some nouns look plural but actually name one person, place, or
thing, and so they're singular:

*The United States is [not **are**] defending its title against the*
United Kingdom. (Although fifty states are in the United States,
it's one country; therefore, you use a singular verb.)

The Everything® Grammar and Style Book *is [not **are**] the best*
grammar book I've ever read! (Even though six words are in the
title, The Everything® Grammar and Style Book *is one book; use*
a singular verb.)

Because I find the subject fascinating, I think it's odd that
*economics is [not **are**] called "the dismal science." (Economics*
looks as if it's a plural word, but since it's one subject it needs a
singular verb.)

Here's another special situation: When you use the words *pants,*
trousers, shears, spectacles, glasses, tongs, and *scissors* alone, you
use a plural verb:

*These pants are [not **is**] too tight since I returned from the cruise.*

*Do [not **Does**] these trousers come in another color?*

But put the words *a pair of* in front of *pants, trousers, shears, spectacles, glasses, tongs,* or *scissors,* and then you need a singular verb:

*This pair of pants is [not **are**] too tight since I returned home from the cruise.*

*Does [not **Do**] this pair of trousers come in another color?*

If you think about it, the logic behind the usage is strange since *pair* means *two,* and *two* denotes a plural. Oh, well . . .

USING COMPOUND SUBJECTS

The first rule in this part is easy. Compound subjects (subjects joined by *and*) take a plural verb:

*Mike and Lynn are [not **is**] here.*

*Mr. and Mrs. Cox are [not **is**] joining us for an informal dinner tonight.*

Here's an exception: If you have two or more subjects joined by *and*—and the subjects are thought of as one unit—then use a singular verb.

*Is [not **Are**] spaghetti and meatballs the special at Rookie's Restaurant today?*

The second rule is *almost* as easy. Singular subjects joined by *or* or *nor* take a singular verb:

*The butcher, the baker, or the candlestick maker is [not **are**] coming to tomorrow's career fair.*

Rule number three is along the same lines as rule number two (and it's also *almost* as easy as the first rule). Plural subjects joined by *or* or *nor* take a plural verb:

*The Paynes or the Meaghers are [not **is**] visiting tonight.*
*The horses or the pigs are [not **is**] making too much noise tonight.*

Did you notice the word *almost* in the second and third rules? The first rule was easy; all you had to do was look at subjects joined by *and*; then use a plural verb. The second and third rules require just a little more thought because you have to be sure that the subjects joined by *or* or *nor* are either *all* singular or *all* plural:

1. If all the subjects are singular, use a singular verb.
2. If all the subjects are plural, use a plural verb.

That covers all the examples in which the subjects are the same, but what if you have one singular subject and one plural subject joined by *or* or *nor*? Do you use a singular or plural verb? Simple: You go by the subject that's closer to the verb. So you would write:

*My cat or my three dogs are [not **is**, since dogs is plural and is closer to the verb] coming with me.*

Or, if you inverted the subjects, you'd write:

*My three dogs or my cat is [not **are**, since cat is singular and is closer to the verb] making me itch.*

HERE, THERE, AND EVERYWHERE

Sometimes writers and speakers have a hard time with sentences that begin with *here* or *there*. Writing either

Here's the money Vincent owes Regina.
or
There's plenty of time left.

is fine because if you changed the contractions into the two words each represents, you'd have "Here is the money Vincent owes Regina" and "There is plenty of time left." No problem, huh? Now look at these sentences:

Here's the books Marsha and Morris said they'd bring.
There's lots of sandwiches left, so help yourself.

In these examples if you change those contractions, you have "Here is the books Marsha and Morris said they'd bring" and "There is lots of sandwiches left, so help yourself." Obviously, you'd never say, "Here is the books" or "There is lots of sandwiches" (you wouldn't, would you?), so the verb form is wrong. Since each of those subjects is plural, you need the plural verb (*are*).

So the rule is this: If you begin a sentence with *here* or *there* and you have a plural subject, be sure to use a plural verb (usually the verb *are*).

INSIDE OUT

In order to provide originality to their sentence structure or to keep their paragraphs from being too monotonous, good writers often change the word order of their sentences from the normal subject-verb pattern. Instead of writing the sentence as in the first example that follows, you might change the word order and present your sentence as it appears in the second example:

The soldiers came over the hill, determined to destroy the fortress.
Over the hill came the soldiers, determined to destroy the fortress.

Both sentences have the subject (*soldiers*) and the verb (*came*), but the second sentence is written in what is called inverted order— the verb before the subject. The caution here is to be sure that the subject agrees with the verb, no matter in what order you write the sentence.

The same rule holds true for questions and for sentences that begin with *here* or *there*:

Here are all my friends in one room.
There go two of my oldest friends!

In both sentences, the normal pattern of subject-verb is reversed. In the first sentence, the subject is *friends* and the verb is *are*. In the second sentence, the subject is *friends* and the verb is *go*.

DO IT! NO, DON'T DO IT!

For some reason, *do*, *does*, *doesn't*, and *don't* are particular problems for certain speakers and writers. Repeat three times: Use *does* and *doesn't* only with singular subjects; use *do* and *don't* only with plural subjects:

*John doesn't [not **don't**] like the new supervisor any more than Linda does.*

*It doesn't [not **don't**] matter if they like him or not; he's here to stay.*

Chapter 9

Constructing Coherent Sentences

You may think, how hard is it to construct a sentence? Many people assume since they know the individual aspects of a sentence all they have to do is put them together and—violà!—they have a perfect sentence. In reality there are several things that can go wrong with sentence construction even if you are versed in the individual elements that make up the sentence. Sentences need to be logical and balanced, they need to be linked by connectors, and they need to avoid things like misplaced modifiers and fragments. This chapter gives you some pointers for looking critically at your sentence construction so that your writing remains solid and clear.

MISPLACED MODIFIERS

The Wrong Place at the Wrong Time

Misplaced modifiers aren't words or phrases that are lost; they're words or phrases that you've put in the wrong place. All of your words—whether they're single words, phrases, or clauses—should be as close as possible to whatever they modify (the words they describe or elaborate on). Take a look at this sentence, written with a single word in the wrong place:

After her wreck, Joanna could comprehend what the ambulance driver was barely saying.

The way the sentence is written, the ambulance driver is barely speaking—but surely that's not what the writer meant. *Barely* is out of its correct place because it modifies the wrong word. It should be moved so that it modifies the verb *could comprehend*. The sentence should be written this way:

After her wreck, Joanna could barely comprehend what the ambulance driver was saying.

In addition to being single words, misplaced modifiers can also be phrases, as in this example:

Witnesses reported that the woman was driving the getaway car with flowing black hair.

How interesting—a car with flowing black hair. *With flowing black hair* is in the wrong place in this sentence (it's misplaced) and should be placed after *woman*. That way, the sentence would read:

Witnesses reported that the woman with flowing black hair was driving the getaway car.

Clauses, too, can be put in the wrong place, as in the following sentence:

Paulette Dixon couldn't stop thinking about her sick baby running in the six-mile road race.

That's quite a baby who can run a six-mile road race (not to mention running while being sick). The clause *running in the six-mile road race* is out of place in this sentence; it should be closer to the noun it modifies (*Paulette Dixon*). The sentence should be reworded this way:

Running in the six-mile road race, Paulette Dixon couldn't stop thinking about her sick baby.

Grammar Facts

A frequent problem often arises with the word *not*. In speaking, we frequently say something like this:

All the chairs in the office are not comfortable for the employees.

The problem with that blanket statement is that the word *not* may be in the wrong place. If the meaning was that some of the chairs were uncomfortable, then the sentence should be reworded this way:

Not all the chairs in the office are comfortable for the employees.

One of the most common problems with misplaced modifiers comes with what are called limiting modifiers—words like *almost*, *even, hardly, just, merely, nearly, only* (the one misplaced most often), *scarcely,* and *simply.* To convey the correct meaning, limiting modifiers must be placed in front of the words they modify.

Take a look at these sentences:

Already, Mr. Goulooze has almost eaten four slabs of ribs!

How does a person almost eat something? Did he have great willpower four different times? Or should the sentence be reworded to say that Mr. Goulooze has eaten almost four slabs of ribs?

Richard has nearly wrecked every car he's had.

Has Richard nearly wrecked the cars—in which case, he should be grateful for his luck—or has he wrecked nearly every car?

DANGLING AND SQUINTING MODIFIERS

Dangling modifiers are another problem in writing and speaking. Dangling modifiers have no word or phrase to describe; they just dangle, or hang, in a sentence without something to hold on to. Look at these sentences:

Long ears drooping on the floor, Julie wondered how the dog could walk.

Is it time for Julie to consider plastic surgery?

While performing, the audience gasped as the singer forgot the words to the song.

Why was the audience performing?

After getting a new paint job, reupholstering was now needed for the car.

Why would reupholstering be painted?

Each of the sentences needs to be reworded so that the modifiers have something to attach to.

Julie wondered how the dog could walk with its long ears drooping on the floor.

The audience gasped as the singer forgot the words to the song while he was performing.

After getting a new paint job, the car needed to be reupholstered.

Another problem comes with squinting modifiers (two-way modifiers). These are words that can logically modify or describe something on either side of them. Take a look at this sentence:

The instructor said after the semester ended that Keevie and Vonda were eligible to retake the test.

What does the phrase *after the semester ended* apply to? Did the instructor *tell* Keevie and Vonda this after the semester ended, or were Keevie and Vonda *eligible* to retake the test after the semester ended? The way this sentence is worded, the meaning isn't clear. To correct this sentence, change the placement of the modifier.

After the semester ended, the instructor said that Keevie and Vonda were eligible to retake the test.

The instructor said that Keevie and Vonda were eligible to retake the test after the semester ended.

PARALLELISM

Balance Is Key

For your work to be easily read—and, in some cases, for it to be coherent—using parallelism is important. This helps you give equality and balance to separate the points you make.

Puzzled? Not to worry. Understanding parallelism isn't as difficult as it may seem. You simply write all the similar parts of a sentence in the same way. If you've used two nouns, you don't suddenly switch to a gerund. If you've used verbs that have a certain tense, you don't suddenly change tenses. If you begin in one voice, you don't suddenly switch to another voice.

Take a look at some of the examples that follow, and you'll get a clearer understanding of what parallelism is and how important it is in your writing.

PARALLELISM PROBLEM 1: ITEMS IN PAIRS OR IN A SERIES

When naming items, you should present them all in the same way. Look at this problem sentence:

This afternoon Doris and Stefanie washed and waxed, and then they were vacuuming the car.

Here is the problem viewed one way:

This afternoon Doris and Stefanie washed (past tense verb) and waxed (past tense verb), and then they were vacuuming (past progressive tense verb) the car.

Here is the problem viewed another way:

This afternoon Doris and Stefanie washed (-ed word) and waxed (-ed word), and then they were vacuuming (-ing word) the car.

Here's the repaired sentence that's now parallel:

This afternoon Doris and Stefanie washed, waxed, and vacuumed the car.

All the verbs are now in the same tense; all verbs are now *-ed* words. The following example shows the incorrect use of parallel items in a series when a colon is used:

A word processor has three helpful features that save time: You can quickly edit material you don't want, you can save drafts and revise them, and it can automatically correct words that you frequently misspell.

Here's the problem viewed one way:

A word processor has three helpful features that save time: You [second person] can quickly edit material you don't want, you [second person] can save drafts and revise them, and it [third person] can automatically correct words that you frequently misspell.

Here's the problem viewed another way:

A word processor has three helpful features that save time: You [you as subject] can quickly edit material you don't want, you [you as subject] can save drafts and revise them, and it [it as subject] can automatically correct words that you frequently misspell.

Here's the repaired sentence that's now parallel:

A word processor has three helpful features that save time: You can quickly edit material you don't want, you can save drafts and revise them, and you can automatically correct words that you frequently misspell.

PARALLELISM PROBLEM 2: CLAUSES

When you're using more than one clause, keep the same voice and use the same type of introduction in each. Here's the problem sentence:

I was worried that Joan would drive too fast, that the road would be too slippery, and that the car would be stopped by the police.

Here's the problem viewed one way:

I was worried that Joan would drive too fast [active voice], that the road would be too slippery [active voice], and that the car would be stopped by the police [passive voice].

Here's the repaired sentence that's now parallel:

I was worried that Joan would drive too fast, that the road would be too slippery, and that the police would stop the car.

PARALLELISM PROBLEM 3: PLACEMENT

Items in a series should be placed in similar locations. Take a look at this problem sentence:

Mike is not only very kind but also is very good-looking.

Let's look at the problem:

Mike is not only [first part of a correlative conjunction not only comes after the verb] very kind but also [second part of a correlative conjunction but also comes before the verb] is very good-looking.

Here's the repaired sentence that's now parallel:

Mike is not only very kind but also very good-looking.

PARALLELISM PROBLEM 4: PLACEMENT OF EMPHASIS OR CHRONOLOGY

If the items in a list have different degrees of importance or if they occur at different times, you should order them according to their emphasis or chronology. Look at this problem sentence:

Misuse of the drug can result in fever, death, or dizziness.

Now, identify the problem:

Misuse of the drug can result in fever [something that's bad], death [something that's the worst of the three], or dizziness [something that's bad].

Here's the repaired sentence that's now parallel:

Misuse of the drug can result in fever, dizziness, or death.

In writing your sentence this way you've built up to the climax (the worst problem—death). You might also include a word or phrase before the last element to add to the buildup; for example, you could word the sentence like this:

Misuse of the drug can result in fever, dizziness, or even death.

PARALLELISM PROBLEM 5: MISSING WORDS

Be sure to include all the words you need for each item in your sentence. Look at this problem sentence:

Coach Tom Todd was honored for guiding his star player Cathy Rymer in her career, her schoolwork, and faith.

Identify the problem:

Coach Tom Todd was honored for guiding his star player Cathy Rymer in her career, her schoolwork, and faith [the word her *is not included in the last item of the list of how the coach guided Rymer].*

Here's the repaired sentence that's now parallel:

Coach Tom Todd was honored for guiding his star player Cathy Rymer in her career, her schoolwork, and her faith.

PARALLELISM PROBLEM 6: UNCLEAR MEANING

Include all the words necessary to indicate the items to which you're referring in the sentence. Look at this problem sentence:

In conducting her interview, Gail Bushrod talked with the college senior and candidate for the job.

Identify the problem: Did Gail talk with one person who was a senior and who was interviewing for the job, or with two people—one of whom was a senior and one of whom was interviewing for the job?

Here's the repaired sentence that's now parallel:

In conducting her interview, Gail Bushrod talked with both the college senior and the candidate for the job.

Grammar Facts

Sometimes you may deliberately repeat certain elements of your sentence, as in this example:

I promise to cut taxes, spending, and exorbitant salary raises.

That sentence is fine the way it is, but to add emphasis to the cuts, you might choose to write it this way:

I promise to cut taxes, to cut spending, and to cut exorbitant salary raises.

PARALLELISM PROBLEM 7: TOO MANY WORDS

You don't need to repeat the same introductory word if it applies to all of the items in your list. Look at this problem sentence:

Bill hopes to see Randa on November 20, December 13, and on January 7.

Identify the problem:

Bill hopes to see Randa on [preposition before noun] November 20, [preposition missing] December 13, and on [preposition appears again] January 7.

Here's the repaired sentence that's now parallel:

Bill hopes to see Randa on November 20, December 13, and January 7.

The same preposition relates to each date, so there is no need to repeat it.

PARALLELISM PROBLEM 8: TOO FEW WORDS

If different prepositions apply to items in a series, be sure to include all the prepositions. Look at this problem sentence:

The ants are on the living room floor, the dining room table, and the sink. (Yikes! Better get out the bug spray!)

Identify the problem:

The ants are on [uses the preposition on with this phrase] the floor, [uses the preposition on with this phrase] the kitchen table, and [uses the preposition on with this phrase, but the preposition should be in] the sink.

Here's the repaired sentence that's now parallel:

The ants are on the living room floor, on the dining room table, and in the sink.

The beginning preposition (*on*) doesn't relate to each area, so you should repeat it in the second phrase and change it to *in* for the third phrase.

PARALLELISM PROBLEM 9: PARALLEL SENTENCES

To add emphasis or smoothness, construct your sentences in a parallel way. Look at this example:

I was nervous and frightened, and I hid my emotions. My sister showed the world that she felt confident and carefree.

Identify the problem: Actually, there's no grammatical problem with the sentences, but they can certainly be improved by being written in a parallel manner.

Here are the repaired sentences that are now parallel:

I was nervous and frightened, and I hid my emotions. My sister was confident and carefree, and she showed the world how she felt.

TIPS FOR PARALLELISM

If a lack of parallelism is often a problem in your writing, try the following tips:

- Look for *-ing* or *-ed* constructions.
- Look for constructions beginning with *it*, *that*, *to*, and *you*.
- Look for constructions beginning with the same preposition.
- Look at the voice (active or passive) used in the constructions.
- Check to see if one of the constructions is more important than the others; if so, place it last.

- If you've used a correlative conjunction, check to see if you have its partner (e.g., *either ... or*).

If you have items in a series, write them down in a column. Look for common elements in two parts of the series, and then convert the other items so they'll be formed in the same way. Sometimes your ear is more reliable than your eye. Good writers read their material aloud and listen for words and phrases that aren't parallel.

LOGICAL SENTENCES

Does It Make Sense?

Making sure your sentences are inherently logical is one of the most important steps in becoming a good writer. You can be quite meticulous in crafting the grammar and punctuation of your sentences and very careful with your spelling and word usage, but if your material has errors in logic, all your hard work will have been for nothing. Lapses in logic can take several different forms. Some are instantly recognizable in a sentence, while others are a little more subtle and, thus, a little more dangerous. Don't let these errors sneak up on you.

FAULTY PREDICATION

Faulty predication (also called illogical predication) is one type of illogical writing. The term *faulty predication* means that your subject and verb don't make sense together—that is, the subject can't "be" or "do" the verb.

Grammar Facts

The illogical uses of *when* and *where* are two of the most common examples of faulty predication. Don't describe a noun or pronoun by using *when* or *where*. Be sure to check your sentence every time (that is, whenever and wherever) you use *when* or *where*.

Take a look at these sentences:

The new breath mint assures customers that it will last all day.
An economics class is when you study monetary and fiscal policy.

In tennis, "playing the net" is where you stand close to the net and hit balls before they bounce.

The reason Felicia Sanners was late was because she had a flat tire.

Each of these sentences has an example of faulty predication. Obviously, a breath mint is incapable of assuring anybody of anything; a class isn't *when* anything; playing the net isn't *where* anything; and a reason isn't *because* anything. Each of these sentences needs to be reworded, perhaps like this:

The makers of the new breath mint assure customers that the mint will last all day.

In an economics class you study monetary and fiscal policy.

In tennis, "playing the net" means you stand close to the net and hit balls before they bounce.

The reason Felicia Sanners was late was that her car had a flat tire.

To check for faulty predication, ask yourself if it's possible for each subject to "do" or "be" the verb. If it's not possible, then change your wording.

FAULTY COORDINATION

Faulty coordination occurs if you join (combine or coordinate) two clauses in an illogical way:

Joey and Micah made their way to the head of the checkout line, yet Joey realized he had forgotten his wallet.

The word *yet* (the word that joins, combines, or coordinates the two clauses) is used incorrectly. The sentence could read:

Joey and Micah made their way to the head of the checkout line, but then Joey realized he had forgotten his wallet.

Another example of faulty coordination comes in sentences that contain independent clauses of unequal importance. The sentences are written in a way that makes the clauses seem equal, as in the following sentence:

David and Kathy paid $50,000 for their new car, and it has tinted glass.

The cost of the car is much more important than the fact that it has tinted glass (at least, it is to most people). To correct the problem, you could make the second clause subordinate to the first (making the second clause an adjective clause).

David and Kathy paid $50,000 for their new car, which has tinted glass.

ABSOLUTE ADJECTIVES

One common problem with comparison occurs when you use absolute adjectives, which are words that—by their definition—can't be compared. Therefore, be sure not to use *more, most, quite, rather, somewhat, very,* and other qualifiers in front of them.

Round, for instance, is one of those words. Something is either round or it's not. Since one thing can't be rounder than something else, *round* is an absolute adjective. Other absolute adjectives include *blank, pure, complete, square, dead, straight, empty, true, eternal,* and *favorite.*

Look at these examples:

The test paper I turned in was somewhat blank.

You can't have a paper that is somewhat blank; either it has something on it or it doesn't.

This is my most favorite restaurant.

Because *favorite* means "at the top of my list," one place can't be more favorite than someplace else.

FAULTY COMPARISONS

Another problem with faulty comparison occurs if you compare two unlike people, places, or things:

The traffic mishaps in April were more numerous than May.

This sentence compares mishaps to May, which makes no sense. The sentence should be rewritten like this:

The traffic mishaps in April were more numerous than those in May.

Take a look at this one:

Jeff Eichholtz decided that the people in Crydonville are friendlier than Park City.

Here people are being compared to a city—obviously, an illogical comparison. The sentence needs to be reworded, perhaps like this:

Jeff Eichholtz came to the conclusion that the people in Crydonville are friendlier than the people in Park City.

Still another problem is an ambiguous comparison, which occurs if you write a statement that could be interpreted two different ways. Look at this sentence:

Dawn dislikes traveling alone more than Dave.

This is an ambiguous comparison because readers aren't sure what the word *more* applies to. Does Dawn dislike traveling alone more than she dislikes Dave, or does she dislike traveling more than Dave does?

SWEEPING GENERALIZATIONS

Sweeping (hasty) generalizations use all-encompassing words like *anyone, everyone, always, never, everything, all, only,* and *none,* and superlatives like *best, greatest, most, least.*

The country never recovers from an economic downturn in just six months.

Be careful with sentences with generalizations like this one. What happens to the writer's credibility if the country does, in fact, recover from a downturn in six months? You're far better off to write in terms of what happens *most of the time* than in terms of what *always* or *never* happens (not to mention that you're protected when you make a mistake). One rewording of the example is this:

The country almost never recovers from an economic downturn in just six months.

Here's another example of a sweeping generalization:

Everyone should strenuously exercise at least thirty minutes a day.

Everyone? Surely a newborn baby or someone who's recovering from surgery shouldn't strenuously exercise. If you reword the sentence, you can leave some room for exceptions or for debate. Here's a rewording that is more reasonable:

Everyone who is able should exercise at least thirty minutes a day.

NON SEQUITURS

A non sequitur is a problem in logic that states an effect that doesn't follow its cause. Put another way, in a non sequitur, the inference or conclusion that you assert doesn't logically follow from what you previously stated.

I turned in a paper; therefore, I'll pass the class.

As any teacher can tell you, the fact that you turned in a paper doesn't necessarily mean you'll pass the class. What if the paper is (a) not on the assigned topic? (b) too short or too long? (c) plagiarized? (d) three weeks late? (e) written on a kindergarten level? In other words, just because one thing happened, the other doesn't necessarily follow. Here are other examples of non sequiturs:

Charlie Buckman has bought products made by Commonwealth Foods for years. The new product, Dog Biscuits for Humans, is bound to be tasty.

Jack Spratt stole a box of paper clips from the office. He probably cheats on his taxes, too.

OMITTED WORDS

Another frequent mistake in logic is to omit *else* or *other* in sentences with comparisons. Read this sentence:

Aunt Lucy likes Louise more than she likes anyone in the family.

The way the sentence is written, Louise isn't in the family. The sentence needs to be reworded this way:

Aunt Lucy likes Louise more than she likes anyone else in the family.

Sometimes sentences need *than* or *as* in order to be logical:

Brent said he could play the guitar as well, if not better than, Jessie.

Taking out the phrase *if not better than* leaves *Brent said he could play the guitar as well Jessie,* a sentence that's obviously incomplete. The sentence should be written with the extra *as* to complete the phrase:

Brent said he could play the guitar as well as, if not better than, Jessie.

LAPSES IN LOGIC

Another type of illogical writing to check for is commonly called *post hoc, ergo propter hoc,* which translates as *after this, so because of this* (also called coincidental correlation). Here the assumption is that because one thing follows another, the first caused the second.

Ashley washed her car in the morning, and the rain started in the afternoon.

The second event wasn't caused by the first: The rain wasn't caused by the car being washed (although, come to think of it, it does seem to rain every time you wash your car, doesn't it?).

If you use a false dilemma (an either/or fallacy), you state that only two alternatives exist, when there are actually more than two.

Whitney Becker can get to her appointment in one of two ways: She can either drive her car or she can walk.

Whitney Becker has other choices: She could call a cab, take the bus, or ask a friend for a ride, so she isn't limited to only two ways of getting to her appointment.

If your argument has a red herring, then it dodges the real issue by citing an irrelevant concern as evidence.

The driver in front of me ran the red light and was speeding, so it's not right that I got a ticket for going 100 mph in a 50 mph zone.

The writer or speaker did something wrong; the fact that the driver ahead did something worse is irrelevant.

If you're guilty of circular reasoning, then your writing has what its name implies—reasoning that goes around in a circle, with nothing substantial in the middle. Here's an example:

The epidemic was dangerous because everyone in town felt unsafe and at risk.

That sentence has no insight because the writer gives no clarification in the second part about why the epidemic was dangerous; the fact that everyone felt unsafe and at risk doesn't explain the danger.

FRAGMENTS

Incomplete Thoughts Confuse Readers

You've been told time and again not to use sentence fragments. Right? (Notice that fragment?) Generally speaking, you shouldn't use fragments because they can confuse your reader, and they sometimes don't get your point across.

How can you recognize fragments? The textbook definition says that a fragment is "a group of words that isn't a sentence." Okay, so what constitutes a sentence? Again, the textbook definition says a sentence is a group of words that (1) has a subject, (2) has a predicate (verb), and (3) expresses a complete thought.

Grammar Facts

Depending on when and where you went to school, you might be more familiar with the definition that says a sentence must form an independent clause. Actually, an independent clause must have a subject, predicate, and complete thought, so the definitions are the same.

If a string of words doesn't have all three of the qualifications (a subject, a verb, and an expression of a complete thought), then you have a fragment rather than a sentence. That's pretty straightforward, don't you think? Take a look at these two words:

Spot ran.

You have a subject *(Spot)*, a verb *(ran)*, and the words express a complete thought; in other words, you don't get confused when you read the two words by themselves. Since you have all the requirements (subject, verb, complete thought), you have a sentence.

Now, look at this group of words:

Although Christian Hazelwood had a new job in a modern office building.

This example is a subordinate clause that's punctuated as if it were a sentence. You have a subject *(Christian Hazelwood)* and a verb *(had)*, but what you don't have is a complete thought. The words serve only to introduce the main idea of the sentence. If someone said only those words to you, you'd be left hanging because you wouldn't know what the main idea was. (Although Christian Hazelwood had a new job—what? He took off for the Far East? He called in sick on his first day? He decided to elope with a billionaire and never have to work again?) The *although* that introduces the sentence means there should be something else to explain the first group of words.

A participial phrase often creates another common sentence fragment. Look at these examples:

Scared stiff by the intense wind and storm.
Going to the beach with her family and friends.

Neither of these groups of words has a main clause to identify who or what is being talked about. Who was scared stiff? Who was going to the beach? Obviously, something's missing.

If you're not sure if the words you've used constitute a sentence, first write them by themselves and then ask yourself if they could be understood without something else being added. If you're still not sure, let them get cold for a while and then reread them. If you're *still* not sure, call a friend and say those particular words and nothing else. You know you have a fragment if your friend says something along the lines of, "And then what?"

Another good way to see if you have a fragment is to take the word group and turn it into a yes-or-no question. If you answer yes to the question, you have a sentence; if you answer no (or if the question makes no sense), you have a fragment. Look at these examples:

Jordan Hill quickly ran back to the shelter of the mansion.

Did Jordan Hill quickly run back to the shelter of the mansion? Yes, he did. Therefore, you have a sentence.

Scared stiff by the intense wind and storm.

Did scared stiff by the intense wind and storm? No, that doesn't make sense. You have a fragment.

Read the following paragraph and see if you can spot the fragments:

The lone woman trudged up the muddy riverbank. Determined that she would make the best of a bad situation. Because of her family's recent run of bad luck. She knew that she had to contribute to the family's finances. That's why she had accepted a teaching position. In this town that was new to her. Impatiently waiting for someone to show her where she was to live. She surveyed the streets and rundown buildings of the little village. Little did she know the problems that she would face in the "wilderness," as she had mentally thought of her new home. First, the schoolhouse wasn't ready. Even though she had written that she wanted to begin classes on the twenty-fourth. The day after her arrival.

Did you spot all the fragments? Take a look at:

Determined that she would make the best of a bad situation.
Because of her family's recent run of bad luck.
In this town that was new to her.

Impatiently waiting for someone to show her where she was to live.
Even though she had written that she wanted to begin classes on
the twenty-fourth.
The day after her arrival.

If you had those words alone on a piece of paper, would anybody know what you meant? No—those words don't form complete thoughts.

How can you correct these fragments? Usually the fragment should be connected to the sentence immediately before or after it—whichever sentence the fragment refers to. (A word of caution: Just be sure that the newly created sentence makes sense.)

The first fragment (*Determined that she would make the best of a bad situation*) can be corrected by hooking it on to the sentence right before it. The corrected sentence should read:

The lone woman trudged up the muddy riverbank, determined that she would make the best of a bad situation.

You could also put the fragment at the beginning of a sentence:

Determined that she would make the best of a bad situation, the lone woman trudged up the muddy riverbank.

Or you could put the fragment inside the sentence:

The lone woman, determined that she would make the best of a bad situation, trudged up the muddy riverbank.

Each of these three new sentences makes sense.

Now, look at the second fragment: *Because of her family's recent run of bad luck.* What about their run of bad luck? Again, if you said those words—and only those words—to someone, you'd get a blank stare; you didn't give the reason behind the *because*. To correct this fragment, you could tack the fragment on to the beginning or middle of the sentence that follows it in the original paragraph:

Because of her family's recent run of bad luck, Elizabeth knew that she had to contribute to the family's finances.

Elizabeth knew that, because of her family's recent run of bad luck, she had to contribute to the family's finances.

By slightly changing some wording (without changing the meaning), you could also add this fragment to the end of the sentence:

Elizabeth knew that she had to contribute to her family's finances because of her parents' recent run of bad luck.

Here's another example of possibilities for rewording a sentence when you incorporate a fragment. Take this fragment and its related sentence:

Impatiently waiting for someone to show her where she was to live. Elizabeth surveyed the streets and rundown buildings of the little village.

You might reword the fragment and sentence and combine them this way:

Elizabeth surveyed the streets and rundown buildings of the little village as she waited impatiently for someone to show her where she was to live.

Another way you might revise is to create an appositive phrase. Take this combination of a sentence and two fragments:

The schoolhouse wasn't ready. Even though Elizabeth Blackwell had written that she wanted to begin classes on the twenty-fourth. The day after her arrival.

It can be rewritten to read:

The schoolhouse wasn't ready even though Elizabeth Blackwell had written that she wanted to begin classes on the twenty-fourth, the day after her arrival.

Here, *the day after her arrival* functions as an appositive phrase.

ACCEPTABLE USES OF FRAGMENTS

Formal writing generally doesn't permit you to use fragments; however, using fragments in casual writing is okay—if they don't confuse your reader. Remember that using fragments (even sparingly) depends on your audience, the restrictions of your instructor or company, and your personal writing style.

Grammar Facts

Remember that you may use fragments if you're quoting someone; in fact, you *must* use fragments if that's what the speaker used.

You might use fragments in short stories or novels (you've started your Great American Novel, haven't you?). A couple rules of thumb are that you shouldn't use them too often, and you shouldn't use them in any way that would puzzle your readers.

Rarely—if ever—should you use a fragment in a news story in a magazine or newspaper. If, however, you're writing an editorial, a fragment might be just what you need to get your point across.

Do we need the new tax law that's on the ballot? Without a doubt.
Will it pass? Probably not.

Both *Without a doubt* and *Probably not* are fragments. But look at how much punch you'd lose if you'd worded that passage and had used complete sentences instead of fragments.

Do we need the new tax law that's on the ballot? Without a doubt
we do. Will it pass? No, it probably will not.

Fragments are also acceptable in bulleted or numbered lists. Take a look at the following example:
Acceptable uses of a fragment include the following:

- When you're quoting someone
- In a bulleted or numbered list
- To make a quick point—but only when the construction isn't confusing to readers

Taken individually, each of the bullets is a fragment, but its meaning is clear. In the type of writing that you do, if you're permitted (or even encouraged) to include bulleted lists, then using fragments is fine.

Grammar Facts

You'll often see fragments as titles, captions, or headings; that's generally acceptable because space restrictions usually won't allow complete sentences. Fragments are also frequently used in advertising. Since fragments are short, readers probably remember them more easily than they would complete sentences.

Sometimes you'll see a fragment intentionally used for emphasis or wry humor. Look at the title of this section and you'll see words that were deliberately constructed as fragments. Also, take a look at this example:

Charlotte Critser quickly told the prospective employer she would never accept a job in a city more than a hundred miles from her hometown. Never. Under no circumstances. For no amount of money. Well, maybe for a new car, an expense account, and double her current salary.

RUN-ON SENTENCES

Where Does One End and Another Begin?

Another mistake in sentence construction is a run-on sentence. The term *run-on* simply means that your sentence has at least two complete thoughts (two independent clauses, if your mind thinks that way), but it lacks the necessary punctuation between the thoughts. This punctuation is needed for readers to know when one thought stops and another begins. Consider the following sentence:

> *The punctuation code gives your readers a signal about where one thought stops and another begins if you don't use some code your readers will be confused.*

Say what? Instead of having the needed punctuation between *begins* and *if*, the sentence, well, "runs on" and its meaning is unclear. (A fairly simple concept, wouldn't you say?)

FUSED SENTENCES AND COMMA SPLICES

One type of run-on, called a fused sentence, occurs when two or more sentences are written (fused) together without a punctuation mark to show readers where the break occurs. Take a look at this sentence:

> *For our annual picnic, Chris Doss and Brad Cummings brought hamburgers we brought potato salad.*

This sentence has two separate thoughts:

> *For our annual picnic, Chris Doss and Brad Cummings brought hamburgers*
> and

we brought potato salad.

This sentence needs some punctuation to tell readers where one thought ends and another begins. You may do this in one of three ways:

1. By creating two separate sentences (For our annual picnic, Chris Doss and Brad Cummings brought hamburgers. We brought potato salad.)
2. By inserting a semicolon (For our annual picnic, Chris Doss and Brad Cummings brought hamburgers; we brought potato salad.)
3. By inserting a comma and one of seven conjunctions—*but, or, yet, so, for, and, nor* (remember *boysfan*?) (For our annual picnic, Chris Doss and Brad Cummings brought hamburgers, and we brought potato salad.)

Grammar Facts

Remember that you must have two (or more) complete thoughts in order to correct a run-on sentence. Ask yourself if each group of words could stand alone (that is, could be a sentence by itself). If one group of words doesn't make sense as a sentence, then you don't have a complete thought.

Another type of run-on is a comma splice (comma fault), a sentence that has two complete thoughts that are joined (spliced together) by just a comma. The problem with a comma splice is that the comma should be replaced by something else—a different punctuation mark, additional words, or both. Take a look at this sentence:

Rachel Johnson wanted to go to the ball game, her friend Kelly Estes wanted to see the new movie.

On either side of the comma, you have a complete thought. The punctuation code says that you need something stronger than just a comma to help readers understand that a thought has been completed.

You have several choices to correct the sentence. You could create two separate sentences by using a period:

Rachel Johnson wanted to go to the ball game. Her friend Kelly Estes wanted to see the new movie.

Another option is to separate the two complete thoughts with a semicolon:

Rachel Johnson wanted to go to the ball game; her friend Kelly Estes wanted to see the new movie.

A third choice is to separate the two complete thoughts with a semicolon and a connecting word or phrase:

Rachel Johnson wanted to go to the ball game; however, her friend Kelly Estes wanted to see the new movie.

Or you could join the two sentences by leaving in the comma but adding one of the seven *boysfan* conjunctions (*but, or, yet, so, for, and, nor*). Of course, you may use the conjunctions only if the sentence makes sense. You may have:

Rachel Johnson wanted to go to the ball game, but her friend Kelly Estes wanted to see the new movie.

Another way you can correct either a fused sentence or a comma splice is to reword the sentence so that one part becomes subordinate (that is, it can't stand alone as a complete thought). Let's look at the first example:

For our annual picnic, Chris Doss and Brad Cummings brought hamburgers we brought potato salad.

You might reword this in a number of ways:

While Chris Doss and Brad Cummings brought hamburgers for our annual picnic, we brought potato salad.
or
Whereas Chris Doss and Brad Cummings brought hamburgers for our annual picnic, we brought potato salad.

Yes, this one sounds really stuffy, and you probably wouldn't use it because of its style—but it does make sense.

Now look at the second example:

Rachel Johnson wanted to go to the ball game, her friend Kelly Estes wanted to see the new movie.

You could rewrite it in this way:

Although Rachel Johnson wanted to go to the ball game, her friend Kelly Estes wanted to see the new movie.
or
While Rachel Johnson wanted to go to the ball game, her friend Kelly Estes wanted to see the new movie.

In each of these examples the first part of the rewritten sentence (the part before the comma) couldn't stand alone as a sentence.

In closing, keep in mind that a sentence doesn't become a run-on merely because of its length. Take a look at this sentence:

At eleven-thirty one Saturday night not long ago, while young Steve Anthren was absentmindedly driving his dilapidated 1953 gray-and-white Chrysler sedan down a lonely, one-lane gravel road that looked as if it hadn't been traversed in many a year, he suddenly glanced in the rearview mirror and was alarmed to see two blinking lights coming from what he supposed was a vehicle of some sort or another; instead of immediately panicking and screaming bloody murder, however, Steve decided that perhaps this signaled a visit from someone from outer space, an alien who would be friendly and would take him to worlds that he had only dreamed of in all of the twenty years of his friendless life.

Although it is basically a nightmare to read (at 117 words, it should be broken into several sentences), it's properly punctuated and isn't a run-on. On either side of the semicolon there's just one complete thought.

Grammar Facts

A comma splice frequently occurs with two quoted sentences, as in this example:

"We're going to the theater at seven," Katrina Rose said "I'd better get dressed right now."

Katrina stated two separate sentences, so you should use either a period (preferable in this case) or a semicolon after *said*.

TRANSITIONAL WORDS AND PHRASES

How Things Connect

Good writers rely on the use of transitional words and phrases. Transitional words and phrases show your readers the association between thoughts, sentences, or paragraphs; plus, they help make your writing smoother.

Sometimes sentences and paragraphs have perfectly constructed grammar, punctuation, and usage, but they lack transitional words or phrases. Material written that way seems awkward and stiff, as in this example:

> *The blind date was a disaster. It was a complete debacle. I was intrigued by what my "friend" Sarah had told me about Bill; she had said he was charming and was open to meeting someone new. He had recently seen me at a party and had wanted to meet me. Sarah said Bill was just my type. She said he was an avid reader; we would have lots to talk about. He liked playing tennis; that was a plus for me.*

There's nothing wrong with the grammar, punctuation, or spelling in that paragraph, but it's choppy and boring. Now read the same paragraph after transitional words and phrases (underlined) have been added:

> *The blind date was <u>more than</u> a disaster. <u>Actually</u>, it was <u>clearly</u> a complete debacle. <u>At first</u>, I was <u>somewhat</u> intrigued by what my "friend" Sarah had told me about Bill; <u>namely</u>, she had said he was <u>quite</u> charming and <u>also</u> was open to meeting someone new. <u>In fact</u>, he had recently seen me <u>in the distance</u> at a party and had wanted to meet me. <u>Besides</u>, Sarah said, Bill was just my type. She said he was <u>quite</u> an avid reader <u>for one thing</u>;*

therefore, we would have lots to talk about. *In addition*, he liked playing tennis; that was *certainly* a plus for me.

Much better, isn't it? By including the transitions, the movement from one idea to another is much smoother, and the language of the paragraph has some life in it.

As important as transitions are in sentences, they're equally important between paragraphs. (Do you see how that transition sentence connects the idea of the preceding paragraph with the idea of this one?) These transitions help you move smoothly from one major concept to the next one.

The following is an excerpt from a piece that compares an essay titled "Why Would You . . . ?" to a personal experience of the writer. Read the two paragraphs and pay particular attention to the first sentence of the second paragraph, the transitional sentence.

> *In Conrad Allen's essay "Why Would You . . . ?" the author recounts how he had been humiliated in elementary school. Allen had been infatuated with Mandy Grayson, a pretty, pigtailed little girl in his class. One Valentine's Day, Allen gave Mandy a card with Manndy perfectly printed—if incorrectly spelled—on the envelope. After she tore open the card, Mandy glanced at it and, much to Conrad's dismay, let it drop on the floor. In a voice loud enough for all the class to hear, she said to Conrad, "Why would you give me a card? You're too dumb and ugly." Allen writes that he first felt his face turn red in embarrassment, and then he felt complete humiliation as the whole class turned around to stare at him to see his reaction. All he could do was stand frozen in front of Mandy, trying in vain to hold back his shame and his tears.*
>
> *Like Allen, I felt shame when I was young. When I was in the fifth grade, my family was undergoing some difficult times. At that age, I was close friends with a group of four other girls; in fact, we called ourselves the "Live Five." Because we all had*

the same teacher, we were able to spend recess and lunchtime together, and we frequently spent the night at each other's houses as well. At one of the sleepovers at my house, the Live Five vowed to stay up all night. Big mistake. In our efforts to keep each other awake, we disturbed my father. That night happened to be one of the many when he was drunk, and he came down to the basement and began cursing and screaming at all of my friends. Not only did he say horrible things to me, but he also yelled at each of my friends and called them terrible names. The shame of that night continues with me today whenever I see one of the Live Five.

Wow, get out the tissues! You probably noticed that the sentence at the beginning of the second paragraph provides a connection between the ideas of the first paragraph and second paragraph. The first two words *(Like Allen)* signal that the main idea of the first paragraph will be continued and that a comparison will be made. Plus, the rest of the sentence *(I felt shame in school)* gives a clue about the topic of the second paragraph. If the transition sentence weren't there, and the second paragraph began *When I was in the fifth grade* …, the second paragraph would seem disjointed from the first, and readers would be confused.

Grammar Facts

Remember that transitional phrases are usually enclosed in commas, unless they're necessary to the meaning of a sentence.

As you can see from these examples (that's another transitional phrase—but you picked up on that, didn't you?), you should add transitions whenever possible to provide necessary links between thoughts and paragraphs. By using them, your writing becomes much more unified and articulate.

CLASSIFYING THE CONNECTORS

Transitional words and phrases can be divided into categories, grouped according to their use. The following should give you lots of ideas for adding transitional elements to your writing:

- **addition/sequence:** additionally, afterward, again, also, another …, besides, finally, first … second … third, further, furthermore, in addition, in the first place, initially, last, later, likewise, meanwhile, moreover, next, other, overall, still, too
- **concession:** admittedly, although it's true that, certainly, conceding that, granted that, in fact, it may appear that, naturally, no doubt, of course, surely, undoubtedly, without a doubt
- **contrast:** after all, alternatively, although, and yet, at the same time, but, conversely, despite, even so, even though, for all that, however, in contrast, in spite of, instead, nevertheless, nonetheless, nor, notwithstanding, on the contrary, on the other hand, or, otherwise, regardless, still, though, yet
- **examples, clarification, emphasis:** after all, an instance of this, as an illustration, by all means, certainly, clearly, definitely, e.g., even, for example, for instance, for one thing, i.e., importantly, indeed, in fact, in other words, in particular, in short, more than that, namely, of course, of major concern, once again, specifically, somewhat, such as, that is, that is to say, the following example, this can be seen in, thus, to clarify, to demonstrate, to illustrate, to repeat, to rephrase, to put another way, truly, undoubtedly, without a doubt
- **place or direction:** above, adjacent to, at that point, below, beyond, close by, closer to, elsewhere, far, farther on, here, in the back, in the distance, in the front, near, nearby, neighboring on, next to, on the other side, opposite to, overhead, there, to the left, to the right, to the side, under, underneath, wherever

- **purpose/cause and effect:** accordingly, as a consequence, as a result, because, consequently, due to, for that reason, for this purpose, hence, in order that, on account of, since, so, so that, then, therefore, thereupon, thus, to do this, to this end, with this in mind, with this objective
- **qualification:** almost, although, always, frequently, habitually, maybe, nearly, never, often, oftentimes, perhaps, probably, time and again
- **result:** accordingly, and so, as a result, as an outcome, consequently, hence, so, then, therefore, thereupon, thus
- **similarity:** again, also, and, as well as, besides, by the same token, for example, furthermore, in a like manner, in a similar way, in the same way, like, likewise, moreover, once more, similarly, so
- **summary or conclusion:** after all, all in all, as a result, as has been noted, as I have said, as we have seen, as mentioned earlier, as stated, clearly, finally, in any event, in brief, in conclusion, in other words, in particular, in short, in simpler terms, in summary, on the whole, that is, therefore, to conclude, to summarize
- **time:** after a bit, after a few days, after a while, afterward, again, also, and then, as long as, as soon as, at first, at last, at length, at that time, at the same time, before, during, earlier, eventually, finally, first, following, formerly, further, hence, initially, immediately, in a few days, in the first place, in the future, in the meantime, in the past, last, lately, later, meanwhile, next, now, on (a certain day), once, presently, previously, recently, second, shortly, simultaneously, since, so far, soon, still, subsequently, then, thereafter, this time, today, tomorrow, until, until now, when, whenever

Chapter 10

Mistakes and Misused Phrases

Clichés, redundancies, and wordiness can clutter your writing. Also, they might distract and annoy your readers, and, perhaps worst of all, they can completely obscure your message. Unoriginal words and phrases make your writing boring and make you lose credibility with your reader. But clichés and redundancies are only a few of the mistakes that can hinder your writing. Using punctuation incorrectly, choosing the wrong word, or switching between points of view are all mistakes that can damage your writing. This chapter will cover the most common grammatical errors in speaking and writing and show you how to avoid them.

CLICHÉS

Overused and Empty

A cliché is a worn-out expression, one you've heard over and over, or time and time again, or a thousand times before (do you get the picture?). It may have been clever or had a special meaning the first time you heard it, but by now you've come across it so many times that it's lost its pizzazz and so doesn't add any spice to your writing.

Grammar Facts

Many clichés are also similes (comparisons using *like* or *as*). You're probably familiar with the following expressions:

- Happy as a lark
- Slippery as an eel
- Pretty as a picture
- Fit as a fiddle
- Blind as a bat
- Snug as a bug in a rug
- Dumb as a post
- High as a kite
- Sharp as a tack

Clichés are phrases that once painted a vivid picture but with overuse the picture they created has faded and become almost meaningless. So while "taking the bull by its horns," may have at one time conjured up an image of an individual going into battle with a bull and winning, now the phrase is throwaway. How to you know if you are using a cliché? Generally if your phrase feels too trendy, if it fails to conjure up a visual image, and if you haven't had to put a lot of thought into what the phrase means, then you might have a cliché and you should try to rewrite the phrase.

As a rule, you should avoid using clichés because they're unoriginal, stale, and monotonous. Your readers won't think your work is the least bit creative if all they see is cliché-ridden writing.

Most likely, you're familiar with hundreds of clichés. When you're getting ideas or writing your first draft, sometimes you'll think of a cliché. Go ahead and write it down. But when you revise your work, get out your eraser (or press the Delete key) pronto and get rid of that cliché.

If you can't think of an original way to reword your cliché, try "translating" it in a literal way. Say, for instance, that you've written:

It was plain as the nose on his face that Corey wouldn't stick his neck out for anybody else.

In that sentence, you're dealing with two clichés *(plain as the nose on his face* and *stick his neck out).* To make the sentence cliché-free, you could change it to:

Plainly, Corey wouldn't take a risk for anybody else.

Is there any time that using a cliché is permissible? Sure. The style for using an occasional cliché is relaxed or casual, so keep in mind that clichés have no place in academic writing. But if your style allows you to use a cliché in a humorous way, go ahead and add one occasionally.

Grammar Facts

It is permissible to use clichés in academic writing if you are quoting someone. You must quote the dialogue exactly in such a case.

The trick is to let your reader know that you're using a cliché intentionally. If you're in a pinch (yes, that's a cliché), write something along the lines of "Even though I knew the cliché 'Little pitchers have big ears,'" and then go on to elaborate as to how the cliché fits in with your topic.

REPETITION AND WORDINESS

I Heard You the First Time

When it comes to writing, using redundant words or phrases not only diminishes the value of your work, but it's also a waste of your reader's time.

Take a look at the following commonly seen or often-heard redundant phrases and read the explanations about why they're redundant. (Get ready to smack yourself on the head as you mutter, "I should have thought of that"—but comfort yourself with the thought that you're certainly not alone in using these phrases!) Then start cutting your own redundancies.

Grammar Facts

Cease and desist. Will and testament. Goods and chattels. Legal documents are rife with redundancies, and the reason goes back to 1066. Before William of Normandy conquered England, English law had commonly been written in Latin and Old English. When William took control of England, Norman French gained stature. However, many people weren't fluent in all three languages. Since lawyers wanted to be certain their documents and proceedings were written precisely and were understood by everyone, they developed phrases that incorporated words with synonyms in Latin, Old English, and Norman French.

REDUNDANT PHRASE	EXPLANATION
advance planning	Planning must be done in advance. Delete *advance*.
A.M. in the morning	A.M. means morning. Delete *in the morning*.
and also	Use one word or the other, but not both.

REDUNDANT PHRASE	EXPLANATION
as an added bonus	If something is a bonus, it must be added. Delete *added*.
ask the question	You can't ask anything except a question; delete *the question*.
ATM machine	The *M* in *ATM* stands for *machine*. Delete *machine*.
basic essentials	If they're the essentials, they have to be basic. Delete *basic*.
cash money	Is cash ever anything but money? Delete *cash*.
close proximity	You can't have far proximity, can you? Delete *close*.
closed fist	A fist must be closed. Delete *closed*.
combined together	Things that are combined must be together. Delete *together*.
completely unanimous	Something cannot be partially unanimous. Delete *completely*.
continue on	Can you continue off? Delete *on*.
cooperate together	You can't cooperate apart. Delete *together*.
each and every	The words mean the same thing; delete one.
end result	Can you have a result that's not in the end? Delete *end*.
estimated at about	Estimated means about. Delete *at about*.
exactly the same	If something is the same, it must be exact. Delete *the same*.
excised out	You can't excise in, can you? Delete *out*.
foreign imports	Material that's imported must be foreign. Delete *foreign*.

REDUNDANT PHRASE	EXPLANATION
free gift (free gratis)	If it's a gift or is gratis, it's free. Delete *free*.
green in color	As opposed to green in what? Delete *in color*.
HIV virus	The *V* in *HIV* stands for *virus*. Delete *virus*.
honest truth	If something isn't the truth, it isn't honest. Delete *honest*.
important essentials	If items are essential, surely they're important. Delete *important*.
large in size	The word *large* denotes size. Delete *in size*.
mutual cooperation	Cooperation has to be mutual. Delete *mutual*.
my own personal opinion	*My opinion* means it's your own and it's personal. Delete *own personal*.
overused cliché	If a phrase isn't overused, it's not a cliché. Delete *overused*.
past memory	You can't have a future memory, can you? Delete *past*.
PIN number	The *N* in *PIN* stands for *number*. Delete *number*.
P.M. at night	P.M. means night. Delete *at night*.
return back	Here again, it's hard to return forward. Delete *back*.
roast beef with au jus	The *au* means *with*; delete *with*.
safe haven	By definition, a haven is a safe place. Delete *safe*.
sudden impulse	An impulse is sudden, or it's not an impulse. Delete *sudden*.

REDUNDANT PHRASE	EXPLANATION
sum total	If you have a sum, you have a total. Delete one word or the other.
totally monopolize	A monopoly is total, isn't it? Delete *totally*.
true fact	By definition, a fact must be true. Delete *true*.
valuable asset	If something is an asset, then it has value. Delete *valuable*.

WORDINESS: LESS IS MORE

Wordiness is the first cousin of redundant writing. If you use six words when two will do, your writing becomes bloated and loses its effectiveness. Wordiness takes up your readers' valuable time, and it can make your writing seem pompous.

Still have your eraser handy or your finger on the Delete key? Take a look at the following list of common wordy expressions; then get to work putting your words on a diet.

WORDY PHRASE	SUGGESTED SUBSTITUTE
a small number of	a few
being of the opinion that	I believe (think)
cannot be avoided	must, should
due to the fact that	since, because
excessive number of	too many
for the purpose of	to, for
give consideration to	consider
has a tendency to	often
last but not least	finally

WORDY PHRASE	SUGGESTED SUBSTITUTE
make an examination of	examine
none at all	none
present time	present, now
the majority of	most
until such time as	until
with regard to	concerning, about

MISUSED PHRASES

Say What You Mean

Sometimes people hear certain nifty or impressive phrases and then later use those same phrases in their own writing or speech. Problems arise when they either misheard the phrase or remembered it incorrectly. What they end up writing or saying is close to the original, but it's not quite right.

The result is often a humorous take on the correct phrase (like a "doggie-dog world" instead of a "dog-eat-dog world"), and sometimes it's just plain puzzling ("beckon call" instead of "beck and call").

The following are some of the more common mistakes of this variety, as reported by copyeditors and teachers.

THE CORRECT PHRASE	WHAT YOU'LL SOMETIMES SEE OR HEAR
all it entails	all it in tails
all of a sudden	all of the sudden
amusing anecdotes	amusing antidotes
beck and call	beckon call
bated breath	baited breath
begging the question	bagging the question
beside the point	besides the point
by accident	on accident
can't fathom it	can't phantom it
down the pike	down the pipe
dyed in the wool	died in the wool
en route to a party	in route (or) in root to a party
far be it from me	far be it for me

THE CORRECT PHRASE	WHAT YOU'LL SOMETIMES SEE OR HEAR
for all intents and purposes	for all intensive purposes
free rein	free reign
got my dander up	got my dandruff up
got his just deserts	got his just desserts
had the wherewithal	had the where with all
home in on	hone in on
I couldn't care less	I could care less
I hope to be at work	hopefully, I'll be at work
in his sights	in his sites
in like Flynn	in like Flint
mind your *p*'s and *q*'s	mind your peas and cues
moot point	mute point
nip it in the bud	nip it in the butt
nuclear power	nucular power
one's surname	one's sir name
out of whack	out of wack
pored over a document	poured over a document
prostate cancer	prostrate cancer
recent poll	recent pole
shoo-in to win	shoe-in to win
supposedly	supposably
take it for granted	take it for granite
the die is cast	the dye is cast
toe the line	towed the line
tongue in cheek	tongue and cheek

THE CORRECT PHRASE	WHAT YOU'LL SOMETIMES SEE OR HEAR
tough row to hoe	tough road to hoe
up and at 'em	up and adam
whet my appetite	wet my appetite

Grammar Facts

One of the most misused phrases is "I could care less." Really "I couldn't care less" is what you should say if you want to express total apathy toward a situation. In this way you are basically saying it would not be possible for me to care less about this situation because I have no care left to give. If you say "I could care less" you are implying that you still have care left you could give.

COMMON GRAMMATICAL MISTAKES

Learn from These Mistakes

In a recent informal survey, copyeditors and English teachers from around the world were asked about mistakes they frequently see in print or speech. Following are some of the results of that survey. Don't feel as if you have to hang your head in shame if you see your own mistakes reported here; the point is to learn from them (and to promise yourself you'll never make them again).

In their responses concerning blunders in written work, the copyeditors tended to focus on errors of grammar, spelling, and usage, while the teachers were inclined to concentrate on the specifics of writing. Following each "complaint" are some suggestions for eliminating these mistakes from your work.

Here are the egregious errors that copyeditors say frequently arise in material they check.

- **Simple misspellings.** If you're working on a computer, send your material through a spell check. Your computer won't catch all of your mistakes (you have to do *some* work yourself), but you'll be surprised at the number of mistakes it does find.
- **Omitted words or words put in the wrong place after cutting and pasting the text.** If, through some great mystery, what you're sure you've written isn't what appears on the page, read, reread, and then (surprise!) reread your material—especially after you've cut and pasted.
- **Using the passive voice when the active voice would be appropriate—and would read better, too.** Look through your completed material for sentences written in the passive voice. Unless there's a particular need for the passive voice, rewrite the sentence in the active voice. (Remember that in the active voice the subject performs the action of the verb.)

- **Improper use of apostrophes (especially plural versus possessive).** Look at each apostrophe you've written and ask yourself if you've used it correctly in a contraction or in showing possession. Pay particular attention to apostrophes used with *yours*, *his*, *hers*, *theirs*, *ours*, *its* (only *it's* ever takes an apostrophe, and only when you mean *it is*).
- **Use of "they" to refer to a singular word (e.g., the child . . . they/their).** Study each *they* in your material and determine which noun it refers to (that is, look at its antecedent). If the noun (the antecedent) is singular, reword your sentence so that the noun is plural, or change *they* to a singular pronoun (*his* or *her*, *he* or *she*, *it*). There is a growing acceptance for the use of the singular *they* (see Chapter 5), especially as a gender-neutral pronoun, so check with your organization's style guide or advocate its use where appropriate.
- **Gratuitous capitalization (sometimes dubbed "decorative capitalization").** Some writers think something is given greater importance or specificity if it's capitalized, even if it isn't a proper noun. Copyeditors say the problem is that writers think anyone or anything that is referred to with some precision seems to get capitalized: job titles (Caseworker, Commissioner, Director), agencies (the Department, the College), or particular fields or programs (Child Welfare, Food Stamps). If you see many capital letters in your writing, take a look at each capitalized word and see if a particular rule applies to it. If not, use lowercase for the word.
- **Comma complaints.** Remember that commas are used for particular reasons, so make sure that you have a reason for each time you used a comma. A few of the transgressions that deal with commas are these: misplaced or omitted commas often resulting in ambiguous sentences; commas inserted between a month and year (September, 2008); commas dropped after parenthetical phrases (such as, "Barack Obama, senator from Illinois said he . . ."); commas misused with restrictive and nonrestrictive

clauses (no commas before *which*; commas before *that* used unnecessarily); commas inserted between the subject and the verb (e.g., "The speeding car, was seen going through a red light"); and commas used too frequently.

- **Number disagreements—either subject-predicate or antecedent-pronoun.** Look for each verb and its subject (or each pronoun and its antecedent); then check to see if *both* of them are singular or *both* of them are plural. If you have a discrepancy, reword your sentence.

- **And the most common error: mistakes in word choice.** If you look through the following list of common mistakes and you recognize ones you often make, look up the correct usage and then develop mnemonics to help you remember. The most common mistakes in word choice are these:

  - Using *which* for *that* and vice versa
  - Using *affect* for *effect* and vice versa
  - Confusing *they're, their,* and *there*
  - Confusing *your* with *you're*
  - Overusing *utilize* (a coined word for this phenomenon: *abutilize*)
  - using *between you and I* instead of *between you and me*
  - Using *compare to* when *compare with* is correct
  - Using *convince someone to* (rather than *persuade someone to*)
  - Using *its* for *it's* and vice versa (the most common mistake)

Grammar Facts

Often people add prefixes to words that don't need them and as a result create nonwords that don't really mean anything. For example, *irregardless* and *unthaw* are not words. *Regardless* and *thaw* by themselves will convey the correct meaning without any useless prefixes.

COMMON WRITING ERRORS

The Writing Is on the Wall

English teachers identified these common problems in writing assignments:

- **Difficulty grasping the concept of a topic sentence.** A topic sentence is the main sentence of the paragraph, one that all other sentences support or elaborate on. Determine your paragraph's topic sentence; then read every other sentence separately and ask yourself if it elaborates on the topic sentence. If it doesn't, eighty-six it.

- **Trouble focusing on the subject at hand.** Go back through your paper and read each sentence separately. Ask yourself if each sentence deals with the topic sentence of its paragraph and also if each sentence relates to your thesis sentence. If you've strayed away from either your topic or your thesis, delete or reword the sentence.

- **No transition from paragraph to paragraph in language or thought.** As you reread your work, locate where you move from one point to another or from one example to another; then use appropriate transitional words or phrases to make a meaningful connection.

- **Inconsistency in verb tense (especially present and past tense).** Go back and determine which tense you've used. Unless you have a reason for a tense change, reword the sentences that change tense.

- **Reliance on the computer's spell check for proofreading.** Although spell checkers are helpful, all they can do is offer suggestions about what you *may* have intended to spell. Using a dictionary, look at the suggested word's definition to be sure that what the checker suggests is in fact the word you intended to write.

- **Comma splices.** For example: "I went to the store, I bought a jug of milk and a six-pack of cola." Review each comma in your work.
- **Sentence fragments.** Read each sentence separately and ask yourself if the words in that sentence make sense when you read them alone. If they don't, your "sentence" is a fragment.
- **Confusion of homophones.** Homophones are words that sound alike but have different meanings and perhaps different spellings, like *to*, *too*, and *two*; *they're*, *their*, and *there*; and *here* and *hear*. Look up the correct usage of the homophones you often misuse, and then develop your own mnemonics to remember them.
- **No sense of who the audience is.** Be sure you're clear about who your intended audience is (that is, to whom or for whom you're writing). Then make sure that each sentence addresses that audience. Common problems arise in the tone used (for instance, don't use language or reasoning that insults people if you're trying to persuade them to your line of thinking) and in addressing someone who isn't part of the audience (for instance, writing "When you take freshman English . . ." when the audience—in this case, the instructor—isn't taking freshman English).
- **Colloquial usages that are inconsistent with the rest of the writing or inappropriate for the type of writing.** Look through your writing for slang words or idiomatic phrases. Unless your work calls for a relaxed or conversational tone (and your instructor or supervisor agrees that tone is necessary), reword your piece and use more formal language.
- **No sentence variation (writing only noun-verb-complement sentences).** Reword some of your sentences so they begin with phrases or dependent clauses. Also try combining two related sentences into one to create less monotonous sentences.
- **Not following directions.** Realize that you're not making up the rules for the assignment, and that—strange as it may seem—your

teacher or supervisor probably has a reason for every direction that he or she has given. Keep the directions in mind as you write a rough draft, and then reread them after you've completed your assignment. If you've "violated" any of the directions, rewrite those parts.

- **Use of generalities instead of specifics.** Your paper must detail any general statements you make. One way to generate details or supporting evidence is to ask *who? what? when? where? why?* and *how?* questions about your topic or thesis sentence.

- **Use of "nonsentences" that have lots of fluff but little substance.** (For example, "Language is important to everyday life and society.") Look for generalizations, clichés, and platitudes in your work. Reword your sentences to be more specific, to be less hackneyed, or to give more details.

- **Point of view that changes (sometimes first person, sometimes third) or is inappropriate (usually second person).** Check each sentence of your manuscript and determine its point of view. If you've changed from one point of view to another without a reason, reword your sentences. Also, check to see if using first- or second-person point of view is permitted (third person is the only point of view allowed in many formats of academic writing).

Appendix

Root Words, Prefixes, and Suffixes

ROOT WORDS

WORD	DEFINITION	EXAMPLES
amo, amor	love, loving, fondness for	amorous, paramour
arch	ancient	archaeology
aster/astra	star	astronomy, astronaut
audio	hear	inaudible, auditorium
bio	life	biology, biography
brev	short	abbreviation, brevity
chron	time	synchronize, chronological
cred, credit	belief, faith, confidence	creditable, credit card
cycle	wheel, circle	motorcycle, tricycle
fix	fasten	suffix, fixative
fortuna	chance, fate, luck	fortune, fortunate
geo	earth	geology, geometry
graph	write/draw	photography, paragraph
hydro	water	hydropower, hydrate
illus	draw, show	illusory, illustrative
legis, leg	law, write	legislature, illegible
log, logue	word, thought	monologue, illogical
nega	deny	negative, negate
op, oper	work	cooperation, operator
path	feeling	pathetic, sympathy, empathy

ROOT WORDS

WORD	DEFINITION	EXAMPLES
phil	love	philosophy, philanthropic
phon	voice, sound	telephone, phonetic
phys	body, nature	physics, physiology
psych	soul, mind	psyche, psychiatric
quar	four	quart, quarto
quint	five	quintet, quintuplet
science	knowledge	conscience, conscientiousness
scrib, script	write	scribble, manuscript
sex	six	sextet, sextuplet
tact	touch	intact, tactile
tele	far off, distant	telephone, television
ten	to hold	tenure, tenant
ter, terr	earth	extraterrestrial, terrain
urb	city	urban, urbane
val	true	valid, invalidate
verb	word	verbal, reverberate

PREFIXES

WORD	DEFINITION	EXAMPLES
a-, an-	without, not	asocial, anachronism
ab-	away, away from	abnormal, abductor
ad-	to, toward, near	adhere, adductor
agri-, agro-	field, soil	agriculture, agroindustrial

PREFIXES

WORD	DEFINITION	EXAMPLES
ambul-	walk, move around	ambulatory, ambulance
ami-, amic-	friend	amicable, amity
amphi-	round, both sides	amphitheater, amphibian
anima-, anim-	life, breath, soul, mind	animate, animal
anni-, annu-	year, yearly	annual, annuity
ante-	before, prior to	antecedent, antebellum
anti-	against	antipathy, anticlimax
aqua-	water	aquarium, aqueous
auto-	self, directed from within	automatic, automated
bi-	two, double	bipartisan, biennial
cardio-	pertaining to the heart	cardiologist, cardiogram
carni-	flesh, meat	carnivorous, carnivore
centi-	one hundred/one hundredth	centigrade, centipede
cinema-	set in motion, movement	cinematography, cinematic
circum-	around, surrounding	circumference, circumspect
co-	with, together, jointly	cooperate, codependent
contra-, counter-	opposed, against	contradict, contrary
corp-, corpus-	body	corpse, corporation
cour-	heart	courage, courageous
cur-	heal, cure	curative, curable

PREFIXES

WORD	DEFINITION	EXAMPLES
curr-, curs-	run, go	curriculum, cursive
de-	away from, downward	dethrone, depart
deca-	ten	decathlon, decahedron
deci-	one tenth	decimal, decimate
dei-, div-	god	deity, divine
demos-	people	democracy, demographic
dent-	teeth	denture, dentist
dia-	across, through	diagonal, diagnosis
dis-	not, apart, reversal	disrespect, disinherit
do-, don-	gift	donation, donor
dominus-	lord	dominant, dominion
dorm-, dormi-	sleeping	dormitory, dormant
duo-, du-	two, a number	duplicate, duologue
dyna-, dyn-	power, strength, force	dynamite, dynamic
dys-	bad, harsh, disordered	dysfunction, dyslexia
eco-	house, household affairs	ecology
ego-	I, self	ego, egomaniac, egocentric
en-, em-	in, into, to cover or contain	encipher, embody
epi-	upon, above, over	epidermis, epitaph
ergo-, erg-	work	ergometer, ergonomics
etym-	truth, true meaning, real	etymology, etymologist
ex-	out of, former	exterior, extract

PREFIXES

WORD	DEFINITION	EXAMPLES
extra-	beyond, outside, external	extracurricular, extramural
fidel-	believe, belief, trust, faith	fidelity
fin-	end, last, limit, boundary	finality, infinity
fluct-	flow, wave	fluctuation, fluctuant
frater-	brother	fraternity, fratricide
grad-	walk, step, move around	graduate, gradual
grav-, griev-	heavy, weighty	gravity, grievous
helio-, heli-	sun	heliocentric, heliostat
hemi-	half	hemisphere, hemistich
hetero-	mixed, different, unlike	heterogeneous, heteronym
homo-	same, alike	homonym, homogeneous
hyper-	above, over, excessive	hyperventilate, hypercritical
hypo-	under, below, less than	hypoglycemia, hypoallergenic
ideo-	idea	ideology, ideal
idio-	one's own	idiom, idiosyncrasy
il-	not, in, into, within	illogical, illiterate
im-	not	impossible, imperceptible
in-	in	incorporate, induction

PREFIXES

WORD	DEFINITION	EXAMPLES
inter-	between, among	interact, Internet
intra-	within, inside	intramural, intravenous
jet-	throw, send, fling, cast, spurt	jettison, jetsam
kilo-	one thousand	kilogram, kilometer
lava-	wash, bathe	lavage, lavatory
lexis-	word	lexicon, lexicography
liber-	free	liberty, liberal
loc-	talk, speak, speech	locution
lumin-, lum-	shine	luminescence, luminaries
luna-	moon, light, shine	lunar, lunatic
macro-	large, great, enlarged	macroeconomics, macrobiotics
magni-, magn-	large, big, great	magnificence, magnify
mal-	bad, ill, wrong, abnormal	maladjusted, malfeasance
mega-	large, great, big, powerful	megavitamin, megalomania
micro-	small, tiny	microscope, microfiche
milli-	one thousandth	millimeter, milligram
mini-, minut-, minu-	small, little	minuscule, miniature
mis-	bad, badly	mistrust, misspell
miso-, mis-	hate, hater, hatred	misogamy, misogyny

PREFIXES

WORD	DEFINITION	EXAMPLES
mono-	one, alone	monocle, monogamy
mor-, mori-	death, dead	mortician, morbid, moribund
multi-	many, much	multinational, multiply
neo-	new, recent, current	neoclassical, neophyte
non-	not	nonessential, nonfiction
oligo-, olig-	few, abnormally small	oligarchy, oligopoly
omni-	all, every	omnipresent, omnipotent
pac-	calm, peaceful	pacify, pacific
pachy-, pach-	thick, dense, large, massive	pachyderm, pachytene
pan-	all, every, completely	pantheistic, pan-American
pater-	father	paternity, patricide
photo-	light	photosynthesis, photoelectric
poly-	many, much, excessive	polygamy, polymorphous
post-	after	postscript, posterior
pre-	before	pregame, prenuptial
pro-	before, in favor of, forward	project, pro-American
pyro-, pyr-	fire, burn	pyromania, pyrotechnics, pyre
re-	restore, back, again	reassemble, redirect

PREFIXES

WORD	DEFINITION	EXAMPLES
retro-	backward, behind, back	retrospective, retrofit
sed-	sit	sedate, sedentary
semi-	twice, half	semiannual, semicolon
soli-, sol-	one, alone, only	solitary, solo
sono-, son-, sona-	sound	sonic, sonance
spec-	see, look, appear, examine	spectator, spectacles
stereo-, stere	solid, firm, three-dimensional	stereograph, stereoscope
sub-	under, beneath	subterranean, subway
super-, supra-, sur-	above, over, excessive	supermodel, surcharge
syn-, sym-	together, with, along with	synchronize, symmetry
tacho-, tach-	fast, swift, rapid acceleration	tachometer, tachyarrhythmia
thermo-, therm-	heat	thermometer, thermostat
trans-	across, on the other side	transport, transatlantic
ultra-	extreme, beyond	ultraconservative, ultralight
un-	not	unsanctioned, unorthodox
uni-	one, single	union, unicycle
xeno-, xen-	foreign, strange	xenophobia, xenolith
zoo-	animal, living being, life	zoology, zoolatry

SUFFIXES

SUFFIX	DEFINITION	EXAMPLES
-able, -ible	able, likely, can do	capable, visible
-ade	act, action	blockade, renegade
-al	characterized by, pertaining to	national, directional
-an, -ian	native of, pertaining to	Martian, Kentuckian, Kenyan
-ance	quality or state of being	protuberance, parlance
-ancy	action, process, condition	hesitancy, infancy
-ant	someone who or something that	observant, savant
-arch	ruler, chief	monarch, matriarch
-ary	related to, connected with	budgetary, planetary
-ation	action, result	syncopation, navigation
-cian	possessing a particular skill	musician, physician
-cide	kill	homicide, pesticide
-cracy	rule	democracy, theocracy
-dom	state of being, realm, office	freedom, wisdom
-ee	one who receives action	employee, refugee
-eer	worker, one who does	auctioneer, profiteer
-en	made of, resembling, become	maiden, harden
-er, -or	one who, that which	weaver, dictator
-ery	skill	bravery, embroidery
-escent	in the process of, becoming	adolescent, quiescent

SUFFIXES

SUFFIX	DEFINITION	EXAMPLES
-esque	in the manner of, resembling	picturesque, Romanesque
-fic	making, causing	terrific, scientific
-ful	full of, characterized by	cheerful, wonderful
-hood	order, quality, state of being	falsehood, brotherhood
-ial	characterized, pertaining to	presidential, industrial
-ify	make, cause	purify, vilify
-ism	condition, manner	feminism, nationalism
-ist	one who, believer, does	elitist, biologist
-itis	inflammation, burning sensation	bursitis, phlebitis
-ity, -ty	state of, quality	captivity, adaptability
-less	without	groundless, penniless
-ment	act of, result, means	disappointment, statement
-ness	quality, degree, state of	forgiveness, happiness
-ology	study of	psychology, ideology
-osis	action, process, condition	hypnosis, tuberculosis
-ous	marked by, having quality of	courteous, fibrous
-phobia	fear of	claustrophobia, agoraphobia
-ship	state, quality	relationship, dictatorship
-wise	in the direction of	clockwise, crosswise
-y	full of	blossomy, muddy

INDEX